M000214341

PSYCHEDELIC SUBURBIA

MARY FINNIGAN

PSYCHEDELIC SUBURBIA

David Bowie and the Beckenham Arts Lab

ISBN-10: 0986377023
ISBN-13: 978-0-9863770-2-0

Library of Congress
Control Number: 2015944966

Cover photo: Ray Stevenson
David Bowie at Flat 1, 24 Foxgrove Road,
Beckenham, August 1969

Cover design: Keith Carlson

Expanded First Edition

Jorvik Press
PMB 424, 5331 SW Macadam Ave., Ste 258,
Portland OR 97239
JorvikPress.com

ABOUT THE AUTHOR

Mary Finnigan was born in Manchester, England just before the start of World War II. Her earliest memories revolve around air raid sirens howling in the night, being dragged out of bed and carried into a shelter in the family dining room. This disturbed start probably contributed to her rebellious nature and the fact that she failed to live up to the expectations loaded onto a young woman in the 1950s.

Marrying an older man at eighteen as an escape route from a controlling mother, she produced two children before bolting from Manchester to London, deserting her husband and landing a job as a fashion writer on the *Daily Mirror*. Her print journalism career included feature writing at the *Daily Sketch, Daily Express* and freelance work at the *Sunday Times*.

During a five-year holiday from the five-day week she met David Bowie. This book tells the story of their adventures together and the legacy from them which is vibrantly alive almost half a century later.

Returning to her journalism career, she worked as a reporter, editor and producer at Visnews, Independent Radio News and the London Broadcasting Company. She now contributes to national newspapers, online publications and BBC radio.

Mary lives in Bristol in the west of England with her partner, Chris Gilchrist. She has three adult offspring and three grand-daughters, is a practising Tibetan Buddhist in the Dzogchen tradition, an active feminist campaigner and an unreconstructed hippie.

ACKNOWLEDGMENTS

The list of people who supported and helped me is long and I apologise for the ones I miss here. For starters there's Chris, who nagged me to get on with it gently and persistently over several years. Then there's my lama, Choegyal Namkhai Norbu, for whom I have deep respect and gratitude – and Peter Stansill, who is both my publisher/editor and long-time friend. This story was written nearly half a century after the events. Mostly I relied on my memory, which is by no means reliable. So if I got anything wrong, misinterpreted situations and forgot things that happened it's entirely my fault and I apologise.

Lots of kind people shared their photos, memories, reminiscences and points of view, including Christina Ostrom, Keith Christmas, Richard Raven, Tony Visconti, Natasha Ryzhova Lau, Dave Walkling, James Plummer, David Bebbington, Ian Anderson, Roger Bacardy, Mark Adams, Craig Hamlin, Chantal Cooke, Lynn Evans Davidson, Alison Fraser Black, Angie Bowie, Lara Owen, Catriona Mundle, Peter Culshaw and Cliff Watkins. Special thanks to Wendy Leigh, Jack (Amory), Iris and Aurora Kane, Bill Liesegang, Ray Stevenson, Caroline Finnigan, Richard Finnigan, the late Peter Finnigan, Daniel Taghioff, Alva Taghioff and (of course) David Bowie. Very special thanks to Wendy Faulkner, whose research skills and enthusiasm were invaluable, and to Paul Kinder for his expert proofing and fact-checking.

Bristol, England and
Valle Gran Rey, La Gomera, Canary Islands
2015

PHOTO CREDITS: DAVID BEBBINGTON (47, 51, 70, 102, 111, 114, 116); WENDY FAULKNER (188, 189), FRANCIS FRITH COLLECTION (4); GAZ DE VERE (173); RAY STEVENSON (COVER, 8, 22); ALVA TAGHIOFF (164); DAVE WALKLING (55, 66, 67); ALLAN WARREN (36); CLIFF WATKINS (159).

*For Chris
With thanks for your love and
the profound pleasure
of your company*

CONTENTS

FOREWORDS

This is the story of something wonderful that happened in a London suburb during the tail end of the 1960s. It is a story that touches on the lives of several famous people, including one iconic musician. But it is mostly a story about a group of people who brought enchantment into a deeply conservative community.

We were young, we were idealistic, talented and irreverent. We were torchbearers for sex 'n' drugs 'n' rock 'n' roll. We did not care about social conventions and we broke many rules, but much to our surprise nearly everyone ended up loving us.

Our influence percolated across south London. More than forty-five years later it is still celebrated as a moment in time when we carried the echoes of the 60s wakeup call into fresh pastures. We planted our seeds on fertile ground because the young people of Beckenham and beyond were ready for change and somehow we also managed to charm their elders. Well, most of them.

Beckenham is an affluent suburb that sits comfortably on the outer fringes of south London. Originally on the northern-most edge of the county of Kent, it became part of the Borough of Bromley in one of several local government realignments instigated with the creation of The Greater London Council in 1965.

Beckenham's history dates back at least to 1086 when it appears in the Domesday Book referred to as Bacheham. This probably means Beohha's village in Anglo Saxon.

Beckenham soon developed into a significant village administered from the Manor House opposite the church.

In 1773 John Cator became Lord of the Manor. When the railway arrived from London in 1857 the Cators realised their estates were ripe for residential development, and soon suburban villas were spreading out from the new station.

Built in the style of an Indian colonial town, with wide tree-lined avenues and large detached houses in generous gardens, they were designed to appeal to the wealthy, looking for a home out of London but convenient for the city. As this market became saturated, the financially astute Cators turned to building smaller properties. Retaining the freehold, they were able to keep control of the development of a sizeable part of the town.

Following World War II, much of the Cator estate was redeveloped with modern houses and flats. This process has continued elsewhere in the town, although some areas remain the same as they were between the two world wars.

Beckenham is overwhelmingly bourgeois and has elected an unbroken lineage of Conservative members of parliament since 1950. It could hardly be described as the perfect location for revolutionary activity, but that is precisely what happened. Not violent revolution, but a revolution of attitudes.

The parental and pensioner generations in Beckenham ought to have been outraged by our activities. Elsewhere in Britain the young people of the 1960s were at loggerheads with their elders. Mums and Dads were in despair over long hair, Afghan waistcoats, rock 'n' roll, free love, demonstrations, dropping out and, most of all, drugs.

In turn, their offspring suffered from extreme incomprehension – they simply did not understand why their lifestyle caused so much anguish. "It's love, peace and freedom man – the things you say you want – so why are you so upset?" All the parents could do was repeat the "get a job" mantra, which to your average hippie was the equivalent of offering them a cup of cold vomit.

But it didn't happen this way during the spring, summer and autumn of 1969 in Beckenham. Maybe the magic had been lying dormant beneath the respectable surface and all we did was tease it into life. Perhaps it was demographic – it occurred because the majority of Beckenham people at that time were mellow and laid back and they did not want to squabble with their kids.

But I suspect it had something to do with the fact that there was an aura of innocence around our manifestations – we were open, naïve and devoid of guile. We wanted to have fun and we wanted everyone else to have a nice time, too.

Beckenham High Street, 1965

BACKGROUND

I am telling this story and I was also part of it. So first I should explain how I came to be a front runner in an extraordinary sequence of events.

I moved from Cheshire to Beckenham in the early 1960s, running away from Peter Finnigan, my first husband. I married him when I was an eighteen-year-old virgin straight out of finishing school in Switzerland and had two children by the time I was twenty-one. I hadn't the faintest idea what I wanted to do with my life.

Peter was a member of a rich and influential Irish Catholic family. They owned department stores in Manchester and London. He was 15 years older than me and desperate to get married after several failed engagements. He was well known in the upper echelons of Cheshire society as a dashing young man with an eye for the girls and was invited to posh parties, hunt balls, horse races, yachting jaunts and so on. He lived in a flat across the hallway from my mother and me, in a converted Victorian mansion in leafy Bowdon – which is more or less a Manchester suburb, but on the outer fringes.

Mother was thrilled to bits when Peter took an interest in me and encouraged our relationship, despite the fact that she must have known he was a weak man who drank too much and was not exactly intellectually gifted. Mother had her own agenda – as a widow running out of money, she too was desperate to get married and was being courted by the deputy town clerk of Wigan. They announced their engagement on the same day as I accepted Peter's proposal. Mother was hugely relieved to get me off her hands into what she believed was a "good match."

To say that I was naïve is an understatement – lamb to the slaughter would be a better description, because marriage to Peter turned out to be a world-class disaster. I think I realised this soon after our honeymoon, but the full extent of it became clear when Peter was sacked from the family business after failing to stand up to his ruthless cousin, Brian. By this time I had two young children – but it became obvious that I was not going to bypass my teens and jump from child to adult. I had some wild oats of my own to sow. London beckoned and I started to plan my escape.

I encountered a hairdresser called Simon Hext when working as a French-to-English translator at a show in Blackpool. Simon had a salon in Beckenham so I invited myself to stay with him and his mother so I could check out accommodation in the London suburbs.

My fairy godmother must have been waving her wand because almost immediately I found Flat 1, 24 Foxgrove Road – a spacious apartment with a big garden in a quiet street close to Beckenham Junction station. It came with a cat called Pywacket and was very affordable at £5 per week. I snapped it up and returned to Bowdon with the news that I was moving to London and taking the kids with me. I spun Peter a story about how it was a good move for both of us, but the reality was that I was leaving him. Poor Peter – I treated him very badly. I tried to make up for this towards the end of his life, but by then he had lost his marbles and probably never noticed my remorse.

The fairy dust was still around after the move. We made the transition to Foxgrove Road with minimal bumps along the way. My daughter Caroline was enrolled in a convent school less than 100 yards down the road and my son Richard got a place at a nursery nearby. The au pair was happy to follow us to London and Peter acquiesced to it all.

With hindsight I realise that I made a headstrong leap into unknown territory, something a more cautious individual would probably have avoided. But I was young, energetic, rebellious and inexperienced, so to me it seemed like release from the constraints of upper middle class decorum, escape from an ill-conceived marriage and from a mother who didn't seem to like me.

I was in my fifties when I found out why I was an embarrassment to my mother. Her sister, my aunt, blurted out one day that I had been brought up under false pretences. It transpired that my natural father was not my mother's husband, who died when I was fourteen, but a Frenchman from the Côte d'Azur. It also emerged that everyone in the family knew about this except me. Maybe my Mediterranean DNA was a subconscious reason why I wanted to run away from the cold, damp northwest of England.

London gave me a magnificent welcome to the job market as well. The *London Evening News* had published a couple of my

freelance features, so when I heard that Ellen Goyder was leaving her job as a fashion writer on the *Daily Mirror* I sent them off to her boss, the formidable Felicity Green. I didn't expect a response but Felicity rang me some days later, invited me for an interview and hired me on the spot. I landed a highly coveted job on the basis of two freelance contributions and Felicity's instincts.

However, there was a problem that I did not immediately recognise. I had zero training or experience in newspaper journalism and there I was working for what was, in the early 1960s, Britain's most successful mass-circulation national daily newspaper.

It was absolutely wonderful for a while, hobnobbing with film stars, models, designers, fashionistas, broadcasters, musicians, and photographers – the icons of Swinging London. They all wanted to know me because what I wrote about them and their activities was read by six million people. But inevitably it ended in tears. My fact checking was sloppy, because I hadn't served my time in the local newspaper salt mines. I made a series of silly mistakes and eventually upset one fashion prima donna so much that Felicity had to sack me.

I bounced back immediately into general feature writing at the long deceased *Daily Sketch*, where I was a lot more careful and a lot happier. My remit was much wider. I wrote about the pianist and conductor Daniel Barenboim when he was in the early days of his brilliant career, I covered the horror of the Aberfan slurry disaster and I flew into Gibraltar in a British plane that was buzzed by Spanish fighter jets during the peak period of the blockade. I interviewed Sharon Tate before she was murdered by Charles Manson.

My newspaper career lasted for several years, but by 1969 I had dropped out of full-time employment. I still did occasional shifts as a freelance for the *Sunday Times*, but mostly lived a contented, relatively idle life as a single mother, enjoying the company of my children. After my regular income and generous Fleet Street expenses vanished, money became a problem. We scraped by one way or another, but opportunities to bring in extra cash were always welcome.

I gave up on staff jobs in 1968, after being busted for possession of a very small amount of herbal cannabis while working on a story about drug trafficking in London. I found my way into a flat in Shepherd's Bush, west London, where wholesale dealing was in progress – a few minutes before a police raid.

I must have upset the fairies, because this stroke of bad luck and bad timing landed me in prison for nine weeks. I was actually given a nine-month sentence after my first lawyer, a Labour MP called John Fraser, whom I'd met while reporting from the House of Commons, bungled my defence.

I fainted into the arms of a prison officer when Mr. Justice Seaton announced: "Finnigan, I am satisfied you were going to take these drugs off the premises. I sentence you to nine months in prison." It seems likely that in 1967 this elderly judge didn't know the difference between the amount of dope in a 35 mm film canister in my handbag and the kilos that were found at the flat. It is also obvious to me now that neither John Fraser nor his managing clerk had any experience of defending people charged with possession of cannabis.

I replaced them with Dean Sargent, a solicitor who came to me via the hippie drug bust organisation, Release. He briefed a barrister called Michael Sherrard who got me out on appeal with an absolute discharge. He offered to waive his fee because of the injustice of what had happened to me.

The Appeal Court judges were equally dismayed and granted me full legal aid. The senior judge, Lord Justice Salmon, said, "This woman should never have been imprisoned, and her solicitors were guilty of gross dereliction of duty." The original solicitor and the barrister he briefed failed to call the most obvious witness – the photographer Harvey Mann, who was working with me on the story. After the judges heard his evidence they turned a leave to appeal hearing into a full-scale appeal against conviction and sentence.

The trauma was over, but its reverberations lasted for several years. At this time post-traumatic stress disorder had not entered popular consciousness. It was what soldiers got after the trenches – not what young women experience after suffering injustice and humiliation. When I first emerged from Hill Hall open prison in Essex I was on an extended high. The exhilaration of release after losing one's freedom is a unique experience – all the more intense for me because of the vindication involved – a mood swing from shock and dismay at being so badly let down by the UK justice system to heartfelt gratitude that some aspects of it functioned effectively.

I cried myself into exhaustion many times in my bleak little cell in Holloway jail for three weeks before I was transferred to Hill Hall. Holloway is everything you have ever heard about the ghastliness of prison life. The regime is brutal, the food barely edible, the conditions medieval and the majority of the inmates are deeply disturbed women – mostly on drug-related offences but also some murderers and gangsters. In 1967 we had to wear hideous prison uniform – the worst aspect of which was the heavy woollen underwear, a nightmare for a fastidious fashionista like me.

There were one or two middle-class women in Holloway, but I learned a lot about proletarian attitudes and behaviour while I was there. There were frequent screams, doors banging and curses day and night, and I saw women being dragged kicking and shouting into solitary by a posse of prison officers.

Many of the officers were bullies with personality disorders of their own, but there was one East European officer, whose name I cannot remember, who became my friend. She had a warm and generous spirit and came to my coming out party, which was hosted by Simon Watson Taylor in Chelsea. Quentin Crisp was among the guests.

I settled into Hill Hall with relief. It was more like a girls' boarding school than a penal institution. In fact I found it a lot easier than most of the inmates because of my boarding school background. The food was a big improvement on Holloway and we sat in foursomes at nicely laid tables with check cloths on them. Hill Hall was an elegant Queen Anne Mansion set in a rural landscape. It was razed to the ground in a fire some years after I left – caused by the relaxed regime which allowed smoking in the dormitories.

I was assigned work with the garden gang. In theory there was an officer with us at all times, but in practice we were often alone for extended periods. It was our job to retrieve the parcels thrown over the wall after visiting time. We stuffed them into our overalls and carried them back to our hut where we were also left alone during tea breaks. We stripped the packaging off the chocolates, sweeties, cigarettes and other goodies and hid the haul in a tea chest where the prison cat slept on a pile of cushions.

The illicit treats were smuggled into the main house in small increments, to be distributed and consumed after lights-out in the dorm. Getting away with this rule-breaking, which could have cost us remission, was the main activity that kept us sane. Dope smoking was rumoured to happen, but I never encountered a spliff.

I was planting tomatoes in one of the greenhouses when the governor's assistant came by with the news that I was free. I threw my bucket of compost into the air and whooped with joy. That evening Rufus Harris from Release and Dean Sergeant, my solicitor, came to collect me. We headed for the nearest pub, where I downed three whiskies in quick succession. Later that night I was reunited with Caroline and Richard and slept in my own bed. The next day my story was all over the newspapers – except for the *Daily Sketch*. From the pub I phoned Vic Treadger, one of my colleagues on the *Sketch* news desk, so he could read the Press Association copy to me. He agreed not to run it – which was a lovely gesture on his part.

As the thrill of release evaporated it was replaced by an uncomfortable period of depression and anxiety. It was not easy to reintegrate into life as a suburban mum. Several journalist colleagues offered me jobs. I accepted one as a feature writer on the *Daily Express* but hated the office culture there. I felt thoroughly out of place and left after a few weeks. With hindsight I know that I was in shock for some time after the prison experience.

During my research into the London drugs scene I met several members of what was then a small psychedelic elite. The majority of 1960s hippies were middle- to upper-class university-educated twenty-somethings. They launched a movement that became known as the London Underground, simultaneously with the cataclysmic social upheavals that originated in San Francisco's Haight-Ashbury district.

I soon realised that my rebellious nature dovetailed neatly with their worldview – which rejected pretty well everything connected with the materialistic black-white, right-wrong "straight" society perspective.

They endorsed a more holistic approach and replaced conventional wisdom with a fresh collection of values drawn from oriental sources like the *I Ching*, the *Bhagavad Gita* and the *Tibetan Book of the Dead* – and occidental ones like William Blake, Jack Kerouac, William Burroughs and Allen Ginsberg.

But most of all they were driven by the profound insights many of us gained from LSD. This was the time when a whole generation of young people discovered drugs, and there were lots of them around – DMT, psilocybin, mescaline, marijuana, opium, amphetamines, Mandrax, Ritalin and more. We all tried one or more of them, but it was LSD that had the most potent effect on our psycho-emotional circuitry and caused us to re-evaluate our priorities.

Out went a mechanistic world view and in came Gaia, with human beings and all life forms integrated into the vibrant totality of planet earth – and its place as a tiny speck in the cosmos.

The drug culture was in its energetic infancy, proclaiming the gospel of love, peace and freedom to all with ears to hear and eyes to see. One aspect of the freedom component mani-fested as cheerfully guilt-free promiscuity. For the first time in human history women had access to reliable birth control via The Pill.

Inspired by the likes of Germaine Greer and Simone de Beauvoir, we burned our bras and passionately embraced sex-ual liberation. I passionately embraced a lot of men and, more by luck than judgement, managed to avoid the 60s plague of gonorrhoea. The most self-righteous hippies spurned alcohol and narcotic "drugs of oblivion," as they called them, while piously advocating "drugs of awareness" – psychedelics and cannabis.

Of course, there was a downside. Many young and beautiful men and women ignored all warnings and lived dangerously, as only the young know how. Some became heroin addicts and only a few survived into middle age. There were LSD casual-ties, like Syd Barrett from the Pink Floyd, who couldn't locate the stop button and never made it back from outer space.

But there were also some very aware, very clever people in our midst, non-addictive personalities with strong survival instincts who managed to avoid body and brain destruction during the initial excitement of the drug bonanza. I had the good fortune to meet many of them.

While I was on bail between my bust and the court appearance, my social life switched from drinking sessions with fellow journalists in Fleet Street pubs to passing joints in sitting rooms draped with Indian cottons, perfumed with incense and with a Ravi Shankar album on the record player.

My new friends included John "Hoppy" Hopkins, who founded the legendary UFO club, London's first psychedelic all-nighter. UFO had a short but glorious life and was succeeded by its clone, Middle Earth. Hoppy was as close as anyone got to being accepted as a leader in alternative London. A legend in his lifetime, Hoppy died in January 2015, a brilliant original thinker and activist who was much loved and much admired. Several newspapers and the BBC carried obituaries.

Other friends ran underground publications (*IT*, *Oz* and *Frendz*), macrobiotic restaurants, avant-garde bookshops, galleries and the Drury Lane Arts Lab. There were actors, artists, poets, architects and musicians.

And as always, since homo sapiens started to tap out rhythms, blow through reeds and tune voices, it was music that united us across the social spectrum – from blue bloods like the Lascelles Brothers, aristos like Nicholas Gormanston and Mark Palmer, to Sid Rawle the tepee man, and Eric the tramp, who lived in the basement of a squat in Kentish Town. One or two of my new friends were somewhat intellectually snobbish, but overall our holistic perspective included a healthy disregard for class and racial distinctions.

This *volte face* in attitudes, insights and behaviour was a lot to take on board for a young journalist from an ultra-conventional background, and it took some time to sink in, especially as I was still in recovery from the prison ordeal. So much change was running in parallel with so many new influences – especially musical ones. My taste was incubated in the classics, but a seismic shift occurred during a stoned encounter with The Byrds. Every cell in my body woke up and danced, and after that I was a rock 'n' roll convert.

I lived with my children in our big flat with a 60-foot garden in Beckenham's Foxgrove Road, in those days a wide, unpaved street complete with potholes, bare earth and gravel. There was very little traffic and the few vehicles that came past moved slowly over the rough surface. Our two cats, Pywacket and Sebastian, sunbathed undisturbed for hours in one or another comfy pothole.

Adjustments had to be made in my relationship with Caroline and Richard. In collusion with my mother, Peter Finnigan decided not to tell them I was in prison. He moved in to look after them, but they were puzzled about my disappearance and not convinced by the vague "she's gone away for a while" answers to their questions.

As a result, there was some explaining to be done when I suddenly reappeared. My intuition under these circumstances is to meet the challenge head on, so I told them the truth in a straightforward manner, which of course generated a raft of queries: "Why did you buy dope?" "Why did you get caught?" "Why weren't we allowed to visit you in prison?" And so on. I told them to address the latter question to Peter, as I set about trying to regain their trust.

Our flat was the ground floor of a large, ugly Victorian mansion that had seen better days. It was a five-minute walk from Beckenham Junction station, which in turn was a twenty-minute ride from central London.

My new friends accepted invitations to visit, so our home soon turned into an outpost of big-city hippiedom. Most of the surrounding residences on Foxgrove Road were elegant detached houses, inhabited by wealthy commuters and their families. My children went to the same fee-paying schools as their children, and for a while we were accepted as respectable citizens.

This changed after my hip epiphany. The coffee morning and cocktail party invitations faded away and I was snubbed in the pub by Simon Hext, whom I'd known when I was still Mrs. Peter Finnigan, a socialite from Cheshire.

I sold a fine antique dining set, replacing it with a home-made revolving table about eighteen inches high, some mattresses and a colourful collection of floor cushions. I bought oriental throws, candles, incense, beads and caftans. A friend went off to India and sold me her amplifier, record deck and speakers. Mozart, Beethoven and Brahms LPs were neglected in favour of a fresh collection including, among others the Rolling Stones, the Beatles, Led Zeppelin, Pink Floyd, the Grateful Dead and, most intensively, Bob Dylan.

My mother, still living up north but a sporadic visitor to her grandchildren, came to us in a state of spluttering indignation. She was outraged by the marriage failure and only grudgingly acknowledged my success as a journalist.

One of her letters included a comment permanently etched into my memory: "We hear that you are frequently in print. Please regularise your private life so we can be wholly proud of you."

Her reaction to the chasm that had opened up between her ideal of me as a dutiful housewife and my current lifestyle was even more extreme. She lambasted me with furious accusations, which of course included diatribes on the hideous consequences of "dabbling in drugs."

When it became obvious that her criticism fell on deaf ears, she called in the Social Services. A social worker turned up, checked us out, spoke to the schools — and we never heard from her again. I didn't care about any of this because life with the counterculture was much more interesting.

In those days there was plenty of high-quality hashish available at moderate prices, most of it imported by enthusiastic amateur smugglers who respected the blessed weed and were righteous about keeping supply lines clear of criminal gangs. One of them, a new friend I'll call Lucy, was a regular visitor to Foxgrove Road. We usually stayed awake till late while she recounted her adventures in Lebanon, Morocco and Turkey. She was especially fond of Ahmed, a shopkeeper in the Tangier souk, who sold the very best pollen hash, hiding it craftily inside metalwork, shoes and other local artefacts.

There were no sniffer dogs around in those days, and Lucy was very good at being invisible. She was my dope guru and, as a result of her initiations, I progressed rapidly from neophyte to connoisseur.

During one of her visits Lucy told me about hip doctors in London who were willing to issue private prescriptions for tincture of cannabis. A leftover from pre-prohibition, it was still listed in the British Pharmacopoeia and available at two pharmacies. It sounded very interesting, mostly because it was legal and one could not be busted for possession. I duly made an appointment with one of the doctors, who scribbled a script for me after a brief consultation. It was all very relaxed, except for the necessary encounter with a granite-faced pharmacist who made her disapproval glaringly obvious.

Later, dedicated potheads persuaded our doctor friends to jettison the alcohol that created the tincture and prescribe us unadulterated extract of cannabis, an extremely potent viscous green gloop. A dip of the tip of one little finger would keep you high for several hours. Inevitably, with that level of prescribing the extract soon ran out and was not replaced.

So ended that short era of legal cannabis consumption. Forty-five years later the country of Uruguay and the US states of Colorado, Washington and Oregon inserted the thin end of the wedge that heralded the beginning of the end of the prohibition that was imposed on the world by racists in the United States government in the 1930s. They did it because weed was the intoxicant of choice among black Americans. The explosion of interest in pot in the western world had as much to do with rebellion against a prejudiced social order as it did with its consciousness-enhancing qualities.

The Finnigan family in 1969

FOREGROUND

April 1969. It is one of those mornings when summer comes early. Under a blue sky and warm sunlight I am pottering in the garden, still in the process of cutting back years of over-grown neglect, pruning, planting and re-modelling. I love gardening, but some observers see an obsession for order and style as symptomatic of a control neurosis. I disagree – and have learned to ignore this type of criticism. I am converting a weed patch into a rose border. It is hard, back-straining work, and soon the lure of the sun lounger becomes irresistible. So too does the bottle of tincture. I lie back, relaxed after my labours, waiting for Dr. Ian's medicine to kick in.

On the top floor of number 24 the window is open and I can hear the domestic life of my friends and neighbours, Christina Ostrom and Barry Jackson. I got to know and like them soon after moving to Beckenham. We share many inter-ests, including books, music and a deep distrust of mainstream politics. Christina is Swedish, an artist and very beautiful. She's a great talker and a good listener, she's funny, warm, engaging, and we have a soul-sister connection.

It is not easy to define Barry. He's from Bromley, he's handsome but somewhat surly, a polar opposite to Christina. Despite spending a lot of time together I feel as if I will never know Barry. Zipped is the word that springs to mind – a common characteristic among middle-class Englishmen.

There's no time pressure in my life at the moment because I am not working, apart from occasional Saturday shifts at *The Sunday Times*. Under the seismic impact of my launch into the Alternative Society I had become disenchanted with newspaper journalism. My new hip-revolutionary friends delivered withering insights into the manipulative propaganda masquerading as news.

"Fear and prejudice," says one of them, a very scary, extremely intelligent individual called Mike Lesser. "Fear to make you stay indoors, prejudice as a divide-and-rule tool."

I realised that horror stories from afar made Mr. and Mrs. Joe Public in the developed world very glad that nothing like this was happening to them. I had learned at the *Daily Sketch* how to write racist copy via innuendo rather than direct reference, so Mike's insight into the *raison d'être* for covert prejudice came as no surprise.

I also realised that the news agenda – events that are acceptable as stories and the ones that aren't – is also designed to dovetail with the interests of a rich and powerful elite. "T'was ever thus," I hear you say. Of course, not a lot has changed since the Penny Dreadfuls became popular with newly literate working-class Victorians.

Thoughts along these lines merge into a pleasantly stoned mental continuum – which expands to include the buzzing of insects, the rustle of leaves – and a realisation that the sounds from Barry and Christina's window have changed.

On the return leg of a long zone-out I become aware of a voice and a guitar making music that is entirely new to me. It is confident, personal and melodious. This, I think, is not your average wannabe rock star. This is something special.

"Who's playing?" I call, as the song ends. A pale, thin face, framed with a halo of curly blonde hair, appears in the open window.

"Hello," he says, politely. "I'm David. Who are you?"

We both smile real smiles, not pretend ones.

"I'm Mary. Would you like a cup of tea and some tincture of cannabis?"

Intrigued, because he'd never heard of tincture, David Bowie plus twelve-string Gibson comes downstairs. We have tea, tincture and biscuits, then cake and a graze from the fridge, and what starts as a brief encounter ends up stretching into evening and night.

As the tincture works its magic we talk, with conversation punctuated by more songs, each one an original composition, the result of David's inspiration and hard work. I learn that he and Barry were school friends. He tells me he's been in the music business for several years and has already released an album, which was not promoted and did not sell.

He has split up with his girlfriend and is living awkwardly with his parents in nearby Bromley. He tells me he sees himself as a radical singer-songwriter but his manager, whose name I'm told is Ken Pitt, wants to turn him into a mainstream pop idol. He's not happy with his manager and he's broke.

"Can you afford a fiver a week? I have a spare room – you can be my lodger if you like."

This impulse flashes into being from who knows where, certainly not my brain because I only met this guy a few hours ago and here I am inviting him to move in.

David says "Yes please." I think I know in my heart that the fiver a week is theoretical and that for him an easy alternative to living at home is an opportunity not to be missed.

He wanders back to Barry and Christina in the small hours and I go to bed wondering what will happen next.

My insecurity turns out to be groundless, because a couple of days later he arrives on the doorstep ready to move in. Today there is just David, a suitcase, the Gibson and a small oblong box. He parks himself on a stool in the kitchen while I make lunch.

"Can I play you a new song?" he asks,

"Yes please."

This is the first time I hear "Space Oddity," and it's my first encounter with a strange instrument called a Stylophone, which seems to have disappeared from the musical landscape, though David did start using it again in 2000. It is a battery-powered electronic device with a keyboard played with a stylus. It sounds like a cross between an organ and a jet engine – and absolutely right for a melancholy song about a space mission gone wrong.

David explains that Space Oddity was written for two voices – his and his friend John Hutchinson's. He tells me that Hutch is a cool guitar player and that he was a member of a mime and music threesome called Feathers. The third member was David's ex-girlfriend, Hermione Farthingale. Feathers disbanded after a short lifespan when David and Hermione split up. David tells me of his plan to perform as a duo with Hutch, but he's not sure it will happen because Hutch's wife, Denise, has other ideas.

To his later deep chagrin, Hutch took his family back to his hometown of Scarborough, leaving David with a solo career and a song that was written for two people. With his usual ingenuity, David got round this problem in live performance by singing one part and playing the other on a tape recorder.

The kids come home from school and are instantly fascinated by the Stylophone. David appears to be completely at ease with Caroline and Richard, explaining how the instrument works and letting them have a go. He plays Space Oddity again and we are unanimous that it's a fabulous song.

"It should go to number one," says Caroline. "I hope it does because I'll be able to impress my school friends."

The refrain about a spaceman floating in a tin can triggers Richard's imagination. He disappears off to the kids' room, to return a while later with a drawing of a spaceman in his capsule, surrounded by the moon, planet earth and various other extra-terrestrial phenomena. David discusses it with Richard, suggesting other things that could be included.

He is an immediate hit with the kids and it becomes clear to all of us that, with David as our lodger, our humdrum suburban life is about to go through a gear change.

David has no money and no gigs, so he spends most of his time in the flat but is by no means idle. I have to admit to myself that when it comes to single-focused dedication, David the musician outranks Mary the journalist by a wide margin.

There is music in our lives throughout the day and frequently far into the night. He composes one new song after another, scribbling lyrics in a notebook and figuring out tunes on the Gibson. We are witnesses to a creative process that goes through stops and starts, hiccups and variations. Then when he feels OK about a song, he asks politely, "What do you think of this?"

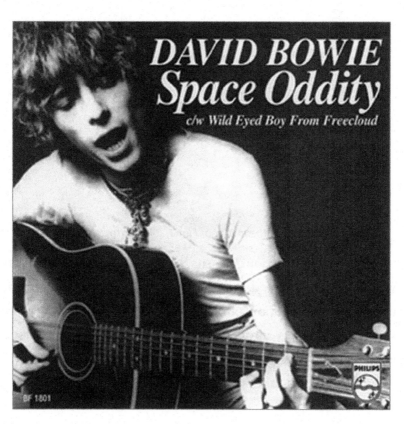

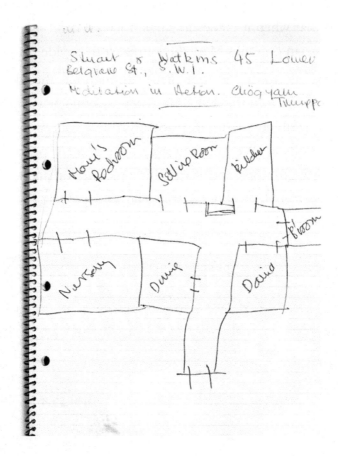

Finnigan's sketch of the layout of Flat 1, 24 Foxgrove Road in 1969.

On warm afternoons he sits on the swing in the garden, working on words and music, usually with one or both of the children messing about around him. "Wild Eyed Boy From Freecloud" comes into being during one of those sessions, inspired by Richard's games. David starts on a song called "The Circling Sponge," especially for Richard, but I doubt it will reach completion.

Sometime after his arrival David expresses concern that Richard is bonding with him. "This could be a problem," he says. I don't see it as a problem, but I should have been more alert. He issues an oblique warning – and I ignore it.

Having David living with us is a new, invigorating experience. I am happy, the kids are happy – none of us at this stage see his presence as transitory.

From the start we do not observe landlady-lodger conventions. I am happy with this arrangement – we share the tincture and Lucy's deliveries of high-quality hashish. We share the space, cook and eat together. And a few days after he moves in David and I sleep together.

The seduction is a work of art and takes me totally by surprise, when I come home one Saturday evening after a shift at the *Sunday Times* (edited in those days by my friend and journalistic mentor, Harry Evans).

Usually I return to a messy kitchen and a sink full of dishes, showing evidence of baked beans, fried egg and tomato ketchup. But on this occasion interesting cooking smells greet my arrival, the kitchen is clean and tidy, with the table laid for two plus flowers, candles and incense. The kids are fed, washed and tucked up in bed.

After a spliff and a nice dinner, David creates a nest of cushions on the floor of his room. He settles me into it and places speakers close to my ears on each side. Then he plays me a selection of his current favourite musical influences.

Some are obscure and some well-known – Jacques Brel, for example, and mind-blowing stereo phasing from Jimi Hendrix.

Snuggled up, stoned and together, inevitably one move leads to another.

David must be confident that he has become an accepted member of the Finnigan household, because early one morning the full impact of his arrival manifests in the form of a friend of his turning up on the doorstep, ready to unload the contents of a dilapidated van.

The friend is in a hurry and I am still half asleep. He squeezes past me carrying two large, battered stage speakers. Two amplifiers land in our narrow hallway, followed by a tape deck, an electric guitar, several mike stands and an assortment of cardboard boxes, loosely packed with leads, plug boards and other assorted musical paraphernalia.

Apart from identifying himself and muttering a surly "Bye then," van man says nothing and leaves as quickly as he arrived.

David is still asleep in my bed.

Caroline emerges from the children's room at the far end of the corridor, late for school and in urgent need of the loo, but her route to the bathroom is now blocked by a vanload of David's professional equipment. Watching carefully where I put my feet, I navigate a path to the point where I can lean forward to lift my daughter and then put her down within reach of the bathroom door.

"This won't work," she complains, and I agree. Apart from other considerations, Caroline is a sturdy eleven-year-old, so hefting her off her feet is not something I want to do on a routine basis. Richard is younger and lighter but also late for school, so that morning there's a repeat performance with him.

David usually sleeps until around midday, but after the kids leave for school it's coffee and wake-up time and, when he's more or less fully conscious, flat reorganisation time.

Initially, most of the gear goes into David's room, but by the time we have packed it all in, it is not easy to move from the door to the bed.

"This isn't going to work," I say – and he agrees.

We take a break, have breakfast and start negotiating. David warned me that he needed his kit. I had agreed to have it in the flat, but until that day I had no concept of how many cumbersome items were involved and how much space they would occupy.

After examining various options I reluctantly accept that the speakers can go in the former dining room, now a chill-out room. They are the bulkiest items and their new location represents a radical re-alignment of my domestic priorities.

The days when I hosted elegant dinner parties were already long gone, but with the advent of David Bowie into our family life, the room where I usually entertain friends is in the process of being transformed into a music studio.

It turns out that the speakers don't stay in their designated location all the time. Sometimes they migrate to the sitting room and sometimes out into the garden, while the amplifiers etc. stay behind. This means that the hallway in between is booby trapped with wiring. This is not dangerous, but is the cause of occasional grumbles from the kids.

How, I hear you ask, did David manage to pull off this takeover? And why was I so docile and compliant?

The answer to question number one is that, even in the early days of our friendship, I was spellbound by his charisma, his charm and his talent. I had been a man-free zone for many months and now there was this handsome, sexy, interesting male creature occupying centre stage in my life – out of the blue and at high velocity.

The answer to the second question is more complex. I was brought up by a mother who indoctrinated me with puritanical values, left over from the Victorian era. Shortly before she died in 1989, I discovered that my mother was in fact a liar and hypocrite, but thirty years earlier, my legacy from her was extreme naïveté coupled with low self-worth. I had only recently discovered feminism and had not yet managed to integrate the principles of gender equality.

At this point in time David was not pushy or rude – he was in fact quite gentle, but he was also a strong character who was used to getting his own way. I was happy to oblige, and not just because of my emotional immaturity.

Being in tandem with David generated excitement, fun, pleasure – and new horizons. There is always an undertone of ambivalence around David's status. Theoretically he is my lodger. But he is also my lover who I naïvely assume to be monogamous. He is seven years younger than me, very horny and sexually sophisticated.

At least once a week he takes the train to London to patrol the folk clubs, looking for work and inspiration. David describes himself as a folkie, but to my ears his songs cannot be pigeonholed.

Living from hand to mouth, he also does casual shifts from time to time at Legastat, a copying office on Carey Street in central London. During these absences he claims he stays with "my friend Calvin." Eventually David tells me more about his friend, Calvin Mark Lee. He is a Chinese-American from California, an A&R man with Mercury Records, and has spotted David's talent.

He was bisexual and, I discovered later, involved with both David and a very pretty young American girl called Mary Angela Barnett.

David also tells me about his love and respect for the mime artist Lindsay Kemp.

Lindsay was David's mime and stagecraft guru for a while and also his lover – but again I did not find out about the physical aspect until much later. Lindsay's influence penetrated everything that David did as a performer for many years.

Lindsay Kemp in 1969

Lindsay occupies the high art end of the entertainment spectrum in a lineage that includes the legendary mime maestros Jean-Louis Barrault and Marcel Marceau.

David and I spend lots of time together in cosy fireside conversations. In one of them I'm surprised when he tells me he's never done LSD. He hints that the prospect of losing control during the psychedelic experience is terrifying.

He mentions his brother Terry's mental illness. "He's schizophrenic and it probably runs in the family."

David's interest in Tibetan Buddhism is another fireside topic. It's familiar territory for me and I am very interested. I'd dipped into Zen meditation, and read *The Tibetan Book of the Dead* after being impressed by Timothy Leary's version of it, *The Psychedelic Experience*.

The non-theistic, contemplative basis of Buddhism was calling me before I met David. I saw it as a logical extension from LSD, but in David's case he bypassed the chemical catalyst.

David tells me about meeting the Tibetan lama Chime Youngdon Rinpoche when, on an impulse, he ducked into the Buddhist Society library to escape a rainstorm.

Chime became David's meditation teacher, mentor and friend. One of only four Tibetan lamas in the UK in 1969, he was a monk in maroon robes, although in common with most lamas who migrated to the west, he disrobed soon afterwards when the temptations of the flesh became irresistible.

David tells me that he used to be serious about Buddhist practice. I have already realised that casual interest is alien to his nature – whatever David does, he does full-on, with concentration and single focus.

Zamsem House (formerly Johnstone House) at Samye Ling

He says that for a while music was on the back burner, when he went to Samye Ling in Dumfriesshire, the first Tibetan dharma centre in the developed world.

He considered being ordained as a monk, he says, but the music would not go away. "On the cushion, it echoed through my meditation, it was with me while out walking in the hills and, sooner rather than too late, I realised I was not being true to myself."

He laughs as he tells me that it was a huge relief when he caught the overnight train from Lockerbie and headed back to show business in London.

In early May, Hutch comes to stay for a few days and adds the dimension of his refined guitar skill to David's compositions. David can strum to useful effect, but he has not learned to finger pick.

I never get to know Hutch well, but on first impression he seems to be a modest, slightly shy individual. He is also in a state of painful indecision – torn between staying in London and pursuing his career with David or yielding to his wife's demand that he return to her and their baby in Scarborough.

David and I do everything we can think of to make Hutch feel comfortable and appreciated, but to no avail.

The disappointment at Hutch's defection gives David the glums for a couple of days. But I have already learned that he's faced setbacks several times since he embarked on his musical career and has so far always managed to bounce back. I am also aware after sharing my life with him for a couple of weeks that attracting attention to your talent in the music business jungle is not an easy task.

At one point during our conversations he says he's envious of the way I landed a job at the *Daily Mirror* with apparently no effort and very little experience.

"Big mistake," I reply, "to leap before you learn. I blew it because I hadn't done my apprenticeship, hadn't learned to fact check as if my life depended on it."

I also learn that David has a lot of friends. People like me who take to him on first encounter and people who have known him since childhood who stay friends. One evening he's been off somewhere and I'm dozing on the sofa. There's a knock at the door – strange because David has a key and I'm not expecting visitors. I open up to find a small crowd on the doorstep, smiling faces and hands clutching bottles and musical instruments. David is front and centre.

"Instant party," he says. "Can we come in?"

I never manage to remember all the names – except for David's best friend, George Underwood, and his girlfriend Janine. George plays guitar but while the party swings along David mentions that George's real talent is visual art.

George addressed the challenge of developing his talent with the same level of single-minded attention that David applied to music. Over the years he polished his work with meticulous attention to detail and in due course created a unique vision. His paintings evoke a spectrum of responses – from discomfort at the surreal, through recognition of a timeless quality to awe at their depth and their beauty. George is now a highly acclaimed artist with a worldwide reputation. His work has been shown at the Royal Academy Summer Exhibition since 1998.

The morning after the party I wake with a slight hangover after drinking more wine than I've done since the advent of hashish into my life. David, however, has a very sore head. He'd been knocking back barley wine, his favourite tipple, which has a very strong alcoholic kick to it.

Reflecting on the beautifully staged seduction and the kind thought behind the instant party, I realise I am falling in love. But there's a big "but," because David has no money and no prospects of getting any well-paid gigs.

I am just about OK with supporting him for a while, but my financial situation is far from brilliant and I have two children to clothe, feed and entertain. My ex, Peter Finnigan, pays their school fees and takes them on holiday but the rest is up to me. As the days pass it becomes obvious that we cannot sustain our lifestyle for much longer. We need an income. Our upstairs neighbours, Barry and Christina, are barely getting by as well.

David falls silent one evening when we are in the upstairs flat and the next day announces: "I've been thinking..."

"Yes," I reply. "I've noticed."

"How about taking a stroll to see if we can find a pub where we can put on a folk club and bring in some cash?" he suggests. "We could do it with Barry and Christina and help them along as well."

We set off around lunchtime when the pubs are open but not crowded. The first one we pass opposite Beckenham Junction Station is dismissed as too brash, too much of a commuter vibe. The next one round the corner in the High Street seems possible but does not have a function room.

The Three Tuns

Then we alight at The Three Tuns, a slightly seedy mock-Tudor building dead centre in the High Street. It's gloomy and old fashioned – in other words, suitably funky. Inside we exchange "this could be it" looks, I order a half pint of cider and David his favourite tipple. We chat up John the landlord, whose personality can best be described as inscrutable.

He responds to our charm offensive in monosyllables but eventually, to our huge delight, agrees to let us have his back room on Sunday evenings.

The landlord must have a kind heart beneath his gruff exterior, because he tells us that at the start we do not have to pay for it.

"I can make a profit on the drink sales," he says.

We inspect the back room. It is dark and dingy and smells of stale beer and cigarettes.

"We'll have to do something to make this cosy," I mutter *sotto voce*.

"Any ideas?" David whispers, with the landlord loitering behind us.

"Sure thing," I reply. "I know how to transform inhospitable dumps."

It's 7.00 pm Sunday 4 May, 1969. We await our first customers at The Three Tuns Folk Club, following a week of feverish activity and stressful suspense. Our big cliff-hanger is how to get the stage gear from Foxgrove Road to the pub. We do not own a car, a taxi is an expensive last resort and the kit is far too big and heavy to hand carry.

David designs and posts an advert for the event outside the pub – and that is the sum total of our publicity.

But the heavens, it seems, are smiling on our endeavour. First the pub landlord and then, just when we are on the edge of despair, there's a knock on the front door on Friday evening.

A delightful woman called Suzy Cartwright stands outside, offering to help out. Suzy runs a mobile hairdressing business and she has a minivan. She tells us she's mad about music, saw the poster and asked around until someone told her where we live. Transport problem solved.

David's professional expertise in the music department is impressive from the start. His gear is battle-scarred by many gigs and clumsy roadies. But he decides on what he needs, tests it and assembles it in a manner that does not create an obstacle course for my children. Naturally they are intrigued by the activity, especially Caroline who has learned to play the Stylophone and is hoping to be invited on stage. And she was, a couple of weeks later. I was misty-eyed as I watched her, so pretty and self-assured, perched on a stool behind a microphone in a red velvet trouser suit playing the Stylophone part in Space Oddity.

It turns out that David is well integrated into a network of folk musicians in London and has no trouble finding a head-line act for our first night. He chooses Tim Hollier, who agrees to perform for a measly fee – which is generous on his part. We have no idea if any, or how many, paying customers will turn up and, as a result, no idea if we will be able to pay him anything.

While David takes care of the music, I get to grips with the décor. On the basis of my experience at the London psyche-delic clubs, I commandeer all our Indian bedspreads, every cushion in the flat and as many San Francisco and Indian post-ers as I can muster. I buy candles and incense and liberate cups and saucers from the kitchen to hold them.

My big hit is an early version of a light projector, lent to me by Barry Lowe, a London friend and psychedelic lightshow artist. I find plain white sheets to hang on the wall behind the stage so I can project a show onto them. Barry has given me a brief tutorial on how to operate his contraption, and now I am on my own.

It works by dripping coloured inks and oil onto glass slides which you sandwich together and slot into a holder on the machine. The powerful lamp inside it heats up the slides and the inks swirl and splat in a glorious colourful display. The clever bit is to know which colours work best together and how much gunk to put in the slides so that the colours stay clear as they move, rather than ending up a muddy mess.

I must have a predisposition for this, because I don't rehearse but get it right on the night.

After forty-six years, my memory is not entirely clear about precisely who did what, where and when at our first night at The Three Tuns. I think David's friend, the record producer Tony Visconti, came and I think he played bass alongside a guitarist friend of his called Rick.

I recall that George Underwood came with Janine and that he did a couple of numbers. I am sure, though, that Barry and Christina were on the door, taking the money – and that about twenty-five people paid five shillings each to get in, which meant that we had enough to pay Tim's train fare with a bit over for his pocket.

Before opening time David sets up the stage while I scurry around with help from Barry and Christina, draping bed sheets on the walls, covering cliché hunting pictures with gaudy posters, lighting candles and incense and moving chairs and tables so we can put cushions on the floor. When I crank the projector into action and we switch off most of the pub lighting, we are really chuffed because we have managed to transform the back room of an English pub into a replica of Haight-Ashbury.

This is my first encounter with David Bowie in live performance. He is charming, professional and at ease – it's obvious that he loves every aspect of being on stage.

Bowie on stage at The Three Tuns during an Arts Lab Sunday

The sound system works fine. He comperes, he plays his own long set, duetting with a tape recorder for Space Oddity, and he tells our small audience about our plans for the club and how it will become a weekly feature of life in Beckenham.

At the end of it all I am up to my armpits in coloured inks – and ecstatically happy. The landlord is concerned about "wacky baccy," but we promise not to allow it indoors. He is impressed with the way we clear up, restoring the back room to its original nondescript status.

We don't make any money, but we don't lose any either. George Underwood, the accomplished artist, agrees to do the following week's poster. He's a fast worker and delivers it to Foxgrove Road on Tuesday morning. It's a big improvement on David's effort. It features a well-known folkie called Keith Christmas as the headline act. Suzy, a voluptuous redhead and a totally lovely person, is delighted to be in on the action and promises her van on a weekly basis.

There's a small queue waiting to get into the back room when we open for business on week two. About fifty paying customers show up that night and with the room well populated there is a buzz in the air – excitement at being in on the start of something new. Something the young people of the suburbs have heard about and perhaps even experienced in London is now happening at walking distance from their parental homes.

The people who turn out to be our core enthusiasts are with us tonight. Most of them are young and, between slide creations, I ask one or two of them how they heard about the club.

"Word of mouth," was the response in common. "My mate saw the poster and came last week. He said it was brilliant."

There are a few older folk music aficionados too. We couldn't fail to notice Chas and Liz Lippeatt. They are thirty-something and formidably eccentric. Chas attracts attention because he seems to be permanently on the verge of a seizure with the intensity of his enthusiasm. He's small, dark and bespectacled and, it transpires, works for the Midland Bank. Liz is large and cheery, less extrovert than her husband. She's an archetypal folkie – long untidy hair, long ethnic patterned skirt, no makeup.

Chas and Liz turn out to be the most steadfast supporters of the Bowie-Beckenham bandwagon. They see it through its several stages and stay active long after David, Barry, Christina and I move on.

And there is the idiosyncratic folk group Comus. It is a folk club tradition that performers wander in off the street to do an impromptu spot. They have to play alongside professionals like David and his fellow big city folkies. If they are awful, they only get to do one or, at most, two numbers.

Comus, however, is welcomed with enthusiasm because they are outstandingly excellent musicians at the avant-garde edge, where popular music meets modern classics. Comus was formed by Roger Wotton who writes the songs, leads the group and performs with passion. Roger's more painfully inspired compositions are a bit much for some members of our audience but mostly they receive appreciative applause. David recognises their talent and invites Comus to become the Folk Club's resident band.

Their female singer is Roger's girlfriend Nita Bowes. She is very attractive, part Indian and comes from a left-wing intellectual family. I make a mental note of her, because she is the first of many young women to flirt with David.

Many years later I was working as a reporter for LBC Radio. One day I was covering an event at County Hall, headquarters of the Greater London Council. The leader, Ken Livingstone, was giving a press conference and was in the middle of a convoluted explanation when Nita and I spotted each other across the crowded room.

We both gave audible squeals and hurried towards each other – a major breach of protocol. We did catch-up when the conference was over. She was Ken Livingstone's personal assistant and had a married name, Nita Clarke. After that she re-materialised as Nita Benn, Special Advisor to New Labour.

The nucleus of what starts as entertainment but is destined to evolve into a social phenomenon comes into being during week two. Chas and Liz and Suzy Cartwright are the front runners, closely followed by tall, handsome Nick Jennings, who wants to be an actor, Mick Weller the poet, and Dave Walkling and James Plummer, who are probably too young to

know what they want. I also have my first encounter with Spud Murphy and the Godwin brothers, Nick and Mick.

If we had lingering doubts around the success or failure of the Folk Club, they are dispelled the following week. Roughly ninety people squeeze into the back room. Certainly most of them heard about us via word of mouth (or perhaps more accurately the psychedelic jungle drums), attracted maybe by the quality of the performances from Keith Christmas – an accomplished guitarist and radical songwriter – and by Comus.

But this is also David's first fan community. His style and charisma are irresistible and so too is his music. It is located somewhere on the leading edge but does not fit into any established category.

David continuously composes new songs. It seems that the success of the Folk Club has given him a fresh burst of creative energy. The music and poetry pour out of him during weekdays at Foxgrove Road, so there is always fresh material ready for The Three Tuns on Sunday.

The atmosphere of a psychedelic happening in the back room of a pub is a powerful magnet. During week three Charles King introduces himself while I am operating the projector. He tells me he and his friend, Stephen Gray, have two, more up-to-date, machines which they would love to offer to the club. I accept with relief, delighted because Barry's projector is on loan and I know he will reclaim it sometime soon. With two projectors operated by two people who know exactly what they are doing, their light shows are sensationally better than mine.

I think it was after week three when the first post-club gatherings took place at the flat. David invited some of his friends back for a jam session and one or two people from the audience tagged along. Thereafter The Three Tuns Folk Club relocated to Foxgrove Road every week after closing time, and the number of people who crammed into my sitting room increased as time went by.

The sessions went on into the small hours, fuelled by spliffs and cups of tea. They were always acoustic, in order not to frighten the neighbours or wake Caroline and Richard, asleep at the far end of the corridor. I regret to this day that it did not cross my mind to record the Foxgrove Road sessions. They would have made fabulous Basement Tapes.

Music at number 24 is acoustic at night – but frequently amplified during daylight hours. This worries me, because I am surrounded by wealthy neighbours living conventional lives in elegant houses. One day I ask David to play with an amp. I walk down Foxgrove Road until I can't hear it. My stroll takes me past Caroline's convent school and almost to the next intersection before the sound fades away. Amazingly, during the entire time David is in residence no-one complains.

Occasionally David rustles up a paid gig. They are rare and usually he takes off by himself with the Gibson. But on one occasion it's a college gig – he needs more apparatus, but paying someone to help him transport it is not an option.

Enter eleven-year-old Caroline Finnigan. "If you can get me off school for a day, I could do it," she says hopefully. It was a no brainer, because I could see she was extremely keen and it would be a big help for David.

So it was that my daughter was roadie for a day for a penniless folkie who eventually became a multi-millionaire show business megastar.

Around this period, when interest in the Folk Club explodes, Flat 1, 24 Foxgrove Road is reconfigured from a family home into the Court of King David. The resident courtiers, Caroline, Richard and myself, are not in the least unhappy about this change in our circumstances. Quite the contrary, in fact, because we are at the epicentre of the action. We are experiencing an entirely new lifestyle, with our home territory now functioning as a creative community.

At first I am overwhelmed by the volume of young, long-haired, dope-smoking, acid-dropping flower children and freaks who arrive on our doorstep, frequently carrying assorted musical instruments. Increasingly they come not only from Beckenham but also from further afield across the south London suburbs – from Orpington, Bromley, Chislehurst, Crystal Palace and Croydon.

Although my role is primarily as tea lady, eventually I relax into the fun of it, especially as it soon becomes clear that several of our day visitors and sofa surfers are willing to take on domestic chores.

This is very useful because David never had any intention of washing dishes, making beds or vacuuming. He occasionally cooks and he can cope with tea and coffee making, but clearing up afterwards is not on his radar.

First among equals in the domestic help department is Kevin "Spud" Murphy. Spud is one of the sweetest, gentlest and most tolerant people I have ever met. He is in his early twenties and smiles at the world from about six-foot-three inches, slightly stooped, ginger-bearded and as thin as a racing snake.

Spud childminding

We learn that he has a serious heart condition and since early childhood has undergone several bouts of major surgery. Spud was never strong enough to do a nine-to-five job. Instead he seems to get satisfaction from being of service to other people. I love Spud and so do many others. Caroline and Richard adore him and he cares for them whenever needed. I confess that I am sometimes impatient with him, but he never complains. He spends more time with us than he does with his own family. I think being with us is his rite of passage from a sheltered, pain-ridden childhood into something not quite, but close to, the adult world – a halfway house, perhaps?

When I heard that Spud's short life came to an end in the mid-1970s, I cried on and off for days. The people who knew him well divvied up to buy and plant a tree in his memory in Beckenham Place Park. I like to think that he fulfilled most of the criteria described in Mahayana Buddhism as the Bodhi-sattva Ideal – individuals, largely free of ego, who forfeit release from suffering in order to incarnate for the benefit of all beings.

Another local personality who I love and admire is our beat bobby, Constable Dennis "Sam" Wheller. Sam came into our lives when I was still a well-paid Fleet Street journalist. We were burgled and I lost some valuable items, which were irreplaceable because I had overlooked to renew our contents insurance. I was incandescent when Sam came to investigate. Somehow he managed to defuse my anger and stayed for tea. During this interlude Janine, my Swiss au pair, returned to the flat after collecting Richard from school. Sam instantly fell head over heels in love with her.

Janine went home to Switzerland when I could no longer afford to pay her, but Sam stayed on as a family friend. When the lifestyle at Foxgrove Road morphs into sex 'n' drugs 'n' rock 'n' roll, Sam remains loyal and unfazed. He is possibly the first police person in the UK to recognise that drug prohibition is a sick joke – unsustainable and unenforceable. Sam drops by from time to time while my flat is populated by dope-smoking musicians and their fans. He clocks that we were fundamentally righteous citizens who are kind to children, pensioners and animals and that we are not criminals. He remarks on the fact that apart from the occasional beer or white wine, we nearly always drink tea.

He comes to a party and totally freaks my London friends, who regard "the fuzz" as the enemy. When I tell him about this sometime later Sam finds it hilarious: "Next time I'll pretend to feel their collars," he says with a raised eyebrow.

Four or five weeks into the lifespan of the Folk Club, David and I realise that we have brought a honeypot into being that attracts not only musicians and music lovers but also diverse creative individuals who want to showcase their talents. Some are passionate about dance, some are wannabe actors, and others are visual artists, filmmakers, writers and poets.

And one especially who stands out as a man with a message the world needs to hear. Brian Moore, the master puppeteer, is a genius with a feeling for the macabre and a talent for expressing it without taking himself seriously. Brian's puppets are weird inhabitants of a dark fantasy realm but they are also funny, somewhat similar to the *commedia dell'arte* but distinctively British. The man himself is painfully shy – he sort of whispers his way into the Folk Club mandala.

Brian went on to a successful career making puppets and sculpting bizarre creations for the BBC, Hollywood, advertising campaigns and animation. He also died young. His daughter, Laylah Moore Fernandez, has created a Facebook page illustrating Brian's work.

Despite the increasing demands on our time and energy from Folk Club fans, David and I still make regular trips to London, sometimes alone and sometimes together. We talk about our London trips, including a recent visit to the Arts Lab in Drury Lane.

The Wikipedia description of this legendary institution, founded by Jim Haynes, goes as follows:

The Lab contained a cinema in the basement designed by Jack Henry Moore and run by David Curtis. In the entrance there was a large gallery space directed by Biddy Peppin (David's girlfriend) and Pamela Zoline. In a separate (but connected) warehouse was the theatre also designed by Jack Henry Moore, who initially co-directed the activities there. Upstairs, the space in front housed a restaurant run by Susan Miles. Haynes lived in the back above the storage and dressing rooms. A number of others lived in various corners of the building, and the all-night cinema was often seen as a cheap crash pad. Such amenities made it perfect for live events and 'happenings' and

helped establish it as the quintessential drop-in/drop-out centre of the
London counterculture. Yoko Ono and John Lennon's first joint artwork
'Build Around' was exhibited at the Arts Lab in May 1968.

By 1969 the Drury Lane Arts Lab resonates so well with the contemporary zeitgeist, it has developed into a movement that is spreading across the UK.

"Maybe we should now re-invent the Folk Club as The Beckenham Arts Lab," I muse.

"Good idea," says David. "I'll float it on Sunday."

We have a packed back room on Sunday night, the 25th of May, which spills over into the conservatory behind it and out into the pub garden. The Strawbs are our headline act and after their set David asks the audience if they would like to turn the club into an Arts Lab. The response is overwhelmingly positive – shouts of approval and a round of applause. Chas Lippeatt is so excited he jumps up and spills his beer into Liz's lap. Spud is grinning like the Cheshire Cat and even the usually laconic Mick Weller is manifesting enthusiasm.

We organised a meeting in the pub garden a few days later to establish the foundations for the Arts Lab. About thirty people turn up, a gathering of colourful young enthusiasts in crushed velvet bell bottoms, floral shirts, ethnic skirts, long hair and headbands. We sit in a circle on the grass. David and I do most of the talking, with Chas chiming in from time to time. At this meeting we decide to call our Arts Lab "Growth."

*Early handwritten lyrics to "Oh! You Pretty Things,"
written in the Finnigan notebook*

In 1969 the word "growth" was not used in the same context as it is in the postmodern world. Back then it represented personal growth and had no connection with economics. In fact, the hippies and freaks of that era were scathing about the parental generation's obsession with material prosperity. Calling someone a "breadhead" was an insult – bread being argot for money in the hip vocabulary inherited from black America, via San Francisco.

Our vision was focused on Timothy Leary's mantra – Tune In, Turn On and Drop Out – in theory, because most of the dropouts were taking time off between school and university. I reckon that ninety-five percent of them ended up married with kids and steady jobs. For us at the time, Growth meant a total recalibration of social priorities.

When Growth was operating at peak voltage my formidably intelligent friend Mike Lesser came to visit.

"There's something extraordinary going on here," he said, while rolling one of his kickass spliffs, picking up with his usual finely tuned antennae that the creative inferno sweeping through London was now apparently fanning out into the suburbs, with equally powerful effect.

Mike was passionate about revolution. His street wisdom and his vision had fuelled the birth of CND and given focus to a raft of hip enterprises. Mike was not on the leading edge – most of the time he invented it. The potential for revolutionary idealism to infiltrate the suburbs made him very happy.

Sadly Mike took his own life in 2015, ending years of suffering with heart disease and lung cancer.

The phenomenon that he encouraged and inspired became known as the Alternative Society – and although it never happened on the grand scale we envisaged, it never entirely disappeared.

Part of it morphed into the New Age movement, but if you know where to look (Ibiza in Spain's Balearic Islands and Valle Gran Rey on the Canary Island La Gomera, for example) you can still encounter unreconstructed hippies. But there is no coherent movement with a passion for creativity and social activism. Usually they are trust fund or social security beneficiaries, or dropouts living rough and dependent on the generosity of others.

Also, many of the ideas and ideals we nurtured and promoted have been absorbed into the mainstream of the way we live today – yoga, mindfulness, sexual liberation, gender and racial equality, health foods and environmental awareness, to quote a few examples. Acid heads like Francis Crick were responsible for outstanding scientific advances.

Soon after the first meeting I volunteer to write a weekly newsletter in collaboration with Nick Godwin, who has access to a copying device known as a duplicator. Processing the copy involves typing it onto wax sheets and the use of volatile, bright pink correcting fluid.

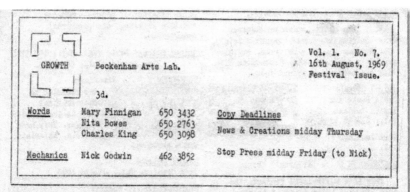

Growth is an Arts Laboratory, Growth is people, Growth is revolution. Growth grows at its own speed, expands according to the energy input it receives, is open to all, but closed to old ideas, cliches, destructive elements and grey thoughts.

Growth started four months ago as a Folk Club at the Three Tuns pub in Beckenham High Street. The first night fifty people turned up to hear David Bowie sing to them. The following week 120 people came to listen and look, one man came with a light machine, and poets, musicians and a tribal-rock group came to entertain...for the fun of it all and instant identification with the vibrations.

From this a creative nucleus was formed and the Arts Lab proper emerged. Mary Finnigan discovered herself as an administrator, Giles Thomas came along with his Train Project, Chas Lippeatt arrived with his films, Stephen Gray and Charles King brought light shows, Michael Weller made us critical of our own efforts and we thrived on it.

Other early supporters, David Mead, Nita Bowes, Davids Jones and Crozier, Nick and Mick Godwin, Chris and Barrie Jackson, Susi Cartwright, joined in the discussions that took place in Mary Finnigan's flat. Somehow the name Growth appeared and the Undergrowth projects were born. Street theatre was the first to get off the ground, followed closely by Barbara Cole and Brian Moore, who brought us their puppet theatre.

Since our small beginnings we have gathered about 200 people into our activities, which now cover 14 different projects...some embryonic, some advanced. (See page 2 for details). There is room for more people, more ideas, more activity.

We are on the verge of acquiring workshop premises but still need a large, permanent roof over our heads. At present our meetings and working parties gather in the homes of our supporters, but this is obviously an unsatisfactory state and the enthusiasm generated so far will only be brought to full flower when we are settled in our own home.

Growth's position as one of the leading Arts Labs has been strengthened by our election to the steering group of the Arts Labs in Great Britain Trust. We are one of nine Labs elected to further a fund-raising campaign for the whole Arts Lab movement.

This Summer Festival and Free Concert is Growth's most ambitious venture to date. Although we trust David Bowie's professionalism to produce polished musical entertainment, we are young and we are novices, so much might appear amateurish in comparison to Blackhill Enterprises or the R.S.P.C.A.

UNDERGROWTH 1 ... Street Theatre.

Will take short, sharp productions into the shopping areas, commuter points, etc. Maximum impact with masks, costumes and basic dialogue. Mini-production hitting the Recreation Ground today.

Spinal Column:
David Bowie and
Angela Barnett.
Tel.: 01-650 3432.

Nick Jennings
Tel: 01-650 8341.

UNDERGROWTH 2 ... Children's Thing.

This is a multi-level project, the most advanced being a puppet theatre. Other plans include taking painting materials into the parks for children, and later music, mime and free expression in a local meeting place. Suggestions for other activities welcome.

Spinal Column:Barry & Christina Jackson,
                Tel.: 01-650 3432.
Mary Finnigan.: 01-650 3432.
Brian Moore & Barbara Cole (Puppets only)
21 Holwood Rd., Bromley. Messages:460 5855

UNDERGROWTH 3 ... Visual Arts.

All forms of painting, drawing, sculpture. Main project is getting 100 pictures into Southern Region trains.

Spinal Column: Giles Thomas, 36 Anerley
                Park, S.E.20.
Michael Weller, Tel.: 01-650 6989.

UNDERGROWTH 4 ... Progressive Music.

Hope to get all musicians who wish to play in large or small groups rehearsing together, writing and performing in varied musical forms. An audition is planned for the near future, no exceptional musical talent required.

Spinal Column: Neil Holmes, 8 Queen
                Adelaide Rd., Penge, S.E.20.

UNDERGROWTH 5 ... Communes.

This group want to find houses where people of like mind can live together in Serenity, Tranquility and Peace.

Spinal Column: Susi Cartwright, Flat 4,
13 Elliott Road, Thornton Heath.

UNDERGROWTH 6 ... Screen Printing.
Aim to set up a workshop and equip it.

Three categories: Growth publicity, creative printing, and commercial commissions.

Spinal Column: David Mead, Tel.: 650 5766
                Nick Godwin, Tel.: 462 3852.

UNDERGROWTH 7 ... Jewellery.
Are planning to produce original W.O.A's in the jewellery medium. They need more tools, materials, and a workshop.

Spinal Column:
Dave Crozier. Tel.: 01-650 4090.

OVERGROWTH 8 ... Poetry.

A poetry group will form when Liz Brookes returns from holiday at the end of August.

UNDERGROWTH 9 ... Light Shows.

Charles King and Stephen Gray have been entertaining us at the Three Tuns since we started, working without pay and minimal expenses. Others have shown interest since in expanding this scene, possible developing it into a travelling show, with money-making potential.

Spinal Column:
Charles King, Tel.: 01-650 3098.
Stephen Gray, Tel.: 01-658 6747.

UNDERGROWTH 10 ... Printed Communications
                    Medium.

We put words onto paper. Too old to call ourselves a newletter, too young to presume a newspaper. Would like to gather word merchants and photographers together for a meeting. Anyone interested please contact:-

Spinal Column:
Mary Finnigan, Tel: 01-650 3432.
Nita Bowes, Tel.: 650 2763.
Charles King, Tel: 650 3098.
Nick Godwin (Production), Tel.: 462 3852.

UNDERGROWTH 11 ... Groovy Movies.

8 mm., off-beat films. Superimposing colour, line drawings etc. Some have already been shown at the Three Tuns.

Spinal Column: Chas Lippeatt, 9 Florence
                Road, Beckenham.

(Continued Page 3.)

It is a laborious operation and I hate doing it but stay with it so that a newsletter appears for distribution on Sunday evenings. Page one of edition number seven is a good example of style and content: "Growth is an Arts Laboratory, Growth is people, Growth is revolution, Growth grows at its own speed, expands according to the energy input it receives, is open to all, but closed to old ideas, clichés, destructive elements and grey thoughts."

The text goes on to describe some familiar, some forgotten, projects that were known as Undergrowths. I have no recall of Giles Thomas's Train Project, for example, and I don't remember Chas's films. I do, however, remember that from the start we needed to fundraise in order to acquire an Arts Lab HQ, so money definitely figured in our ambitions. The hugely popular Sunday nights generated a meagre income split between two households, but it was little more than pocket money and certainly not enough to save up to rent premises.

There is lots of enthusiasm at the first meeting for David's ideas about Street Theatre, to be performed along Beckenham High Street on Saturday mornings, when the maximum number of shoppers are out and about. The aim is part enjoyment, part propaganda – alternative lifestyle enthusiasts are always keen to proselytise.

Rehearsals for the street theatre production are held in Beckenham Place Park. Dog-walkers stop to gaze in wonder at a group of long-haired men and women strutting their theatrical stuff. David sits cross-legged on the grass, directing his cast.

The production that hit Beckenham High Street the following Saturday seals our fate with the older generations. I am not involved in this escapade but hear from those who are that they're worried about how it will shake down. It might be seen as an outrage and we might lose The Three Tuns as a result. On the other hand it may be received as a slice of harmless youthful exuberance.

Sighs of relief all round when David and the wannabe thespians return wearing their crude makeup and amateur dramatic-type costumes – and huge smiles. The good folk of Beckenham, it transpires, are enchanted with the spectacle. Not only does it generate a round of applause outside the supermarket, but also several people ask for a repeat performance.

It is a warm, dry summer. Sunny days stretch into long, crepuscular evenings. I am content bordering on complacent, which should have been a wake-up call. But if it was there, I did not heed it.

David snoozing with Pywacket, the Finnigan cat

Bowie and friends
at street theatre rehearsals
in Beckenham Place Park.

TURBULENCE

Turbulence is gathering momentum, but when it hits it comes as a shocking surprise.

Opening the front door of the flat after a few days away, my nose registers change. Sniff – a whiff of furniture polish. Sniff again – disinfectant over a Chanel base note. And not even the faintest odours of what might have been expected. Sweaty socks for example, take-away curry and the usual ever-present blend of fag ends and cannabis smoke.

Into the kitchen, and my eyes confirm what my nose had detected. It is spotless. The sink is empty and shiny, the work-tops are immaculate, the floor gleams and there's not a dirty mug or spoon in sight. I pause to take in this astonishing turn of events, because it is almost beyond belief. I had braced myself before my return to the horror of the kitchen sink, the time I would spend scrubbing congealed Vindaloo off the cooker and the overall domestic grunge that usually greets my return after a few days away.

Now there I am, with nothing to do except gawp and speculate over a range of possibilities. David has finally noticed the squalor that accumulates when I disappear from the household and has hired a home help. Spud or one of the other Arts Lab people has come by and cleaned up before I return. Then comes a flash of intuition. I move noiselessly towards David's room, give the door the smallest possible shove and poke my face round it.

The bed is made, the room is clean, tidy and empty. The Chanel smell is stronger, a flowered silk kimono hangs over a chair and on the window ledge I find David's latest song, scribbled on a spiral notebook.

Mary Angela Barnett

It starts with the words "beautiful Angie" and goes on into an outpouring of praise and passion. It is not one of his best and I never hear it performed, but it gives me the message with devastating clarity. I retreat into the kitchen in a state of bewilderment, thoughts charging over how I would cope with my next encounter with David – and my first with the woman who has usurped my position in his life.

Even under the cool scrutiny of 20/20 hindsight, I have to admit that I was in love with David. Well, the limited sort of love I was capable of in those days, but hindsight also tells me that with David I went through a quantum shift in my capacity to love and so, proportionately, my capacity to be hurt and jealous.

As the numbness of shock recedes, it is replaced by extreme mortification. Who is this paragon who is beautiful, sexy and house-trained? How could David be so cruel to me, bringing a new woman into my home while I am away? Lost love stereotypes bounce up one after another until, inevitably, I burst into tears and beat my fists against the Formica. Then I go to bed and fall into a fidgety, insecure sleep.

Sometime later I become aware of my nose again. It tells me that lunch is ready – and that lunch is different. Normal Bowie fare is a fry-up and burnt toast. Unless set to seduce or impress, the man is not interested in gastronomic subtlety. Food is more like fuel to keep the music going, to be tossed onto plate and into mouth as fast as possible and with minimal attention.

That day, however, someone is concocting something clever with cheese and garlic. As I stumble out of bed, it comes to me – of course, she has to be a good cook as well.

Chords that later become "An Occasional Dream" reverberate from the kitchen. A female voice with an American accent enthuses, "Honey that's great."

Then, as my presence is felt, she turns from the cooker and, without a second's hesitation or a flicker of embarrassment, manifests an enormous smile and moves towards me, hand outstretched.

"Hi Mary, I'm so happy to meet you. David has told me wonderful things about you."

Disarming, charming and probably insincere, but I am easily led and still befuddled with sleep, and allow myself to be steered into the sitting room and fed delicious pasta and salad washed down with chilled Frascati.

Not only has Mary Angela Barnett (at age nineteen, ten years my junior) ousted me from David's bed, but she has also managed to replace me in my own kitchen.

Even when restored to full consciousness and revived with several puffs of good Moroccan, I sit back, as docile as a newborn puppy and allow Angie to roam free, centre stage. She is tall, slim and graceful with showgirl legs and a long, thick mane of mouse-blond hair. I watch her face carefully, trying to decide if she really is beautiful. The eyes are big and perfectly set. The nose and chin are chiselled and perfectly proportioned. The mouth however, is less than perfect. It is big – too big. And loud – too loud.

She keeps talking, flattering me and probing for common ground. I learn that, like me, she was at school in Switzerland and speaks fluent French. Unlike me, she is the adored daughter of wealthy parents. She is expensively dressed in impeccable casual style and good taste. She exudes confidence, wit, kindness and friendship.

She seems to be blessed with advantages most of us only dream about, and as I watch her, so winsomely entertaining and energetic, I feel my self-esteem ebbing away. In a matter of minutes Angie reigns supreme in the Court of King David.

She is street-wise beyond her years, very clever and, I suspect, quite cunning too. Perhaps she really does like me and feels some remorse about stealing David.

I have an open mind about this, because many years later she confessed that she had been seeing David as her boyfriend for about the same length of time as I had known him – and that he never told her he was romancing me. I get confirmation of this, also many years later, from Tim Goffe, who told me that Angie had a room in the flat in London he shared with Bob Harris – and that David was a regular overnight visitor.

From that time onwards Angie more or less moves in, sharing David's single bed and small room. She disappears for

David and Angie after their wedding at Bromley Register Office, 1970

a day or two from time to time, returning with clean clothes and a shopping bag full of tasty food. No one asks me if it's OK for her to join the household and David keeps a low profile during this transition, offering no apology, no explanation and no comfort.

For a while I am extremely miserable. I feel betrayed but also helpless to do anything about it. He gives the impression that jilting a girlfriend and simultaneously moving in her replacement is no big deal. It is a big deal for me and alone in my bed I cry a lot.

I have to admit, though, that I enjoy Angie's company. It is a refreshing change from the gangly youths who leave roaches in the ashtrays and guitar-string booby traps. More than anything else, though, I am putty in Angie's hands because she is so bloody wonderful around the house.

My children like her, too. She makes them laugh, takes them out for treats and buys them expensive luxuries. Caroline is on the cusp between childhood and adolescence, so she adores Angie's sophistication and the indiscreet stories tossed around about the sex lives of the rich and famous. Caroline's eyes pop at the mention of Mick Jagger, Marc Bolan and Bob Dylan. I spot the gleam in them too, as she thinks about her rise in the school pecking order when she relays such delicious gossip to her friends.

Angie throws herself a hundred percent into everything that goes on around David. She keeps a room in London but spends most of her time with us in Beckenham, doing more than a fair quota of the domestic chores. I find myself accepting her and, remarkably quickly, the pain of rejection subsides.

We cook together and mostly speak French in the kitchen, which irritates David because he doesn't understand it and feels left out. To retaliate, he perches on a stool with the Gibson and distracts us with new song lines.

All this added up to quite an achievement for Angie. Within a very short time she has attracted a gorgeous, talented boyfriend, displaced her rival and then moved in on both of them.

As the ex, I should have been furious and thrown them both out, but I wasn't and I didn't because life was still funny, bizarre and exciting with them around – even if my mother keeps screaming at me on the phone, threatening to report me to the Social Services again for being a selfish and irresponsible parent.

The fun continues without hiccups for a while, until one day David returns from London, ashen-faced and minus Angie.

"What's up?" I asked

"She had hysterics in the train and got out at Kent House. I've been walking around for hours but I can't find her."

Kent House is the stop before Beckenham Junction and plumb centre of a vast, featureless suburban sprawl. Someone who has lived in south London all their life would have difficulty navigating through it, so for an American, brought up in

Cyprus, Angie's escapade was the equivalent of jumping off a river boat in the Amazon jungle.

We sit glumly, wondering what to do next, but we are underestimating Angie. After a while there's a knock on the door. David and I both make a dash, but I get there first. It is Angie, standing between two policemen who have silly grins on their faces. She strides in, apparently unscathed, steering the cops along with her.

"These guys gave me a ride," she announces. "And now I'm going to give them a cup of tea."

I shoot David a piercing glance as I stand in the corridor, blocking their passage – and manage to conceal my relief when he gets the message and vanishes to hide the stash, empty the ashtray and open a window.

A few days later she throws another hissy fit, just before the main act during a Three Tuns night. David is away, so Angie and I are managing the gig between us, with Barry and Christina on the door. Angie is crying and shouting and storming around the car park, refusing to say why she is upset. Then the main act, Keith Christmas, who returns by popular demand, comes out to find Angie, who is supposed to be compering the show. She melts into his arms and, as she does so, gives me a wink.

So it continues – a few days of light-hearted peace and quiet and then another emotional upheaval. When all her cylinders are firing evenly I had to keep on reminding myself that Angie is only nineteen, but when she goes ballistic it is disturbingly obvious that her apparent maturity is skin deep. With what soon becomes predictable regularity, she throws tantrums whenever she is not the centre of attention. She also throws carefully calculated tantrums, stage-managed to bend people to her will, confuse a perceived enemy or, I realise after the Keith Christmas incident, seduce anyone who takes her fancy.

I am very slow on the uptake around the complexities of David and Angie's sex life. Eventually I clock that David had been bisexually multi-timing me for the duration of our physical togetherness. This is the first in series of wake up calls that make me question what I am doing with my life.

I have no doubts about my role as a front runner with The Beckenham Arts Lab. It is a wonderful, pioneering phenomenon, which is cloning itself into a multiplicity of creative directions. The people who are part of it do dangerous things, like smoking dope, taking LSD and treating sex as recreation, but they are a conventional bunch when viewed in comparison with Angie.

After a while I realise she is carrying serious decadence into our midst and that David Bowie, the lad from the south London suburbs, has been on the lookout for someone like her to catalyse him into that world. Do I want to extend my boundaries any further or should I retreat while I still can? Child welfare figures prominently in these deliberations.

Eventually it is Angie, part angel, part hellcat, who provides the solution to this dilemma, when she sets out with unshakeable determination to seduce me.

I guess Angie is testing her acting skills – and my potential as a lesbian lover. Which way, if at all, would I bounce? First off she tries the butch approach. One evening when David is away she emerges from his room dressed in a tweed suit – with her hair scraped into a knot at the back of her neck. The outfit includes a shirt and tie.

She invites me out for dinner, so we stroll together down Beckenham High Street, attracting curious glances from passing suburbanites. If they are hip to what's going on, they are faster off the mark than I am. One hundred per cent inexperienced in the realm of same-sex flirtation, I am puzzled by the outfit but too shy to mention it and oblivious to her intentions.

The penny drops the following night. I come home to find Angie pouting prettily and draped over the sitting room sofa, dressed in a Regency-style ball gown, with her hair in ringlets, face made up and cleavage very much in evidence – the femme approach this time.

I am flattered that she is going to so much trouble to entice me but also terrified of the implications. Even if having a romp with Angie might lead to a threesome with David, it is almost too much for the remnants of my conventional mindset. Too bewildering, too alien, too challenging.

Confused by a tsunami of conflicting emotions, I allow her to steer me into my bedroom. The encounter is a failure. Angie does her best to please me, but I am incapable of responding.

This doesn't seem to bother Angie and we remain house-mates and friends. There's not even any embarrassment, so I figure she probably shrugs it off as a nice try and probably did it with a genuine intention to please me. Even after our short acquaintance I become aware that Angie is a bundle of contradictions.

Life at court and at The Three Tuns carries on as before. Every Sunday before The Three Tuns, one or two Arts Lab devotees usually turn up at Foxgrove Road to help carry the gear.

On one Sunday Nick Jennings, Angie and I are hanging out in David's room while he rehearses with the Gibson. Gradually the power and intensity of his playing increases, to the point where he seems to be possessed by an energy that comes from beyond the human realm. There are words to the song, but they are spontaneous and, as far as I know, never repeated or written down. He improvises effortlessly, fluently and bril-liantly. I never hear David play like this again. We are awestruck witnesses to moments of sublime inspiration.

We are a bunch of anarchic, stoned hippies but there is appreciation for what we are doing with The Arts Lab across a broad spectrum of Beckenham life. The street theatre with Brian Moore's puppets, music, dance, exotic costumes and Angie's loud, outrageous American voice bring a taste of boho into the Saturday shopping routine. The sound, light and laughter that spills out from The Three Tuns every Sunday brings sparkle into the last weekend hours before the Monday commute to work.

One day we have a surprising request from an unusual source. A very nice, elegant middle-aged woman from the Bromley Arts Centre visits Foxgrove Road with an invitation to perform at their headquarters. The Arts Lab, experimental by nature and spontaneous in its manifestations, apparently gives us credibility with the Bromley arts establishment. They own a large detached house and ask us to do a gig there once a fortnight.

We persuade Suzy to drive a posse of us to Bromley – and, after inspecting the place, we're at a loss to figure out how to respond.

It is very posh, with acres of polished wood flooring, oriental rugs, dainty gilt chairs and a concert grand piano. This represents a total contrast to The Three Tuns, with its rickety old stage gear, beer, cigarettes, incense, marijuana (in the garden) and messy light projectors.

Back home, we think long and deep about someone or something respectable we could put on in Bromley.

"Why not ask Chime to talk about Buddhism?" I suggest.

"That's not art," someone retorts.

Then David springs into life. "Hang on a minute," he says. "If we put Chime on first, then Comus, it might work."

Comus are acoustic, they come from middle-class homes, look clean and tidy, do not smoke dope on stage and although usually intense and sometimes strident, they can be relied on not to shock – not totally reliable, but almost. They are the closest we can get to respectability and to art.

I hover within listening distance while David talks to Chime on the phone. One end of the conversation seems to be going well. David is respectful, pitches the request without undue emphasis – but even so I am astonished when he tells me that Chime has agreed to our proposition.

My view of Tibetan lamas in those days was tinged with awe. I saw them as remote beings, living austere lives, who occasionally deigned to talk to naive westerners and to accept our adulation. By the time we started the Bromley gigs I knew that David was a cut above your average folk rocker and he notched up another hit of kudos by attracting a real live Rinpoche into our midst. Rinpoche means "Precious One" and is an honorific accorded to lamas who are recognised as reincarnations of their predecessors.

It really was a remarkable achievement, because not only did Chime Rinpoche come to Bromley, but he also travelled from and to his home in Streatham by public transport. Nowadays lamas of Chime's stature are whisked around in limos. In 1969 Chime was a red-robed monk.

At the Bromley Arts Centre Chime Rinpoche, a tall, thin lama from eastern Tibet, stands in front of a puzzled audience and speaks about wisdom and compassion – the core principles of Mahayana Buddhism. A predominantly middle-aged white Anglo-Saxon gathering sits on the gilt chairs, trying to make sense of what's going on. It is almost certainly the first time many of them have heard of a Tibetan lama, let alone encountering one in person.

Chime tells us about the life of the historical Buddha, Gautama Sakyamuni and about how Buddhism spread from India into Tibet. There's a rustle of surprise from our audience when he states that Buddhism is based in a principle called "dependent origination" and does not accept the existence of a creator God. Then he mentions meditation.

"What is meditation?" asks an elderly lady in the front row. Chime giggles, the lady is fazed and we who are responsible for this enormous break with convention shift uneasily on our chairs.

"It is like waking up," he says, "like discovering your real nature."

If Chime had been anything other than an accomplished meditation teacher, the evening would have flopped beyond redemption at this point. But his authenticity is palpable, his charm mesmerising and his sense of humour mightily infectious. Many of us understand something that night that makes us wonder about what is missing in our lives.

Comus play an inspired set. There is fire and passion in Roger's voice, softened with something that might have been humility. They even manage a few light-hearted moments, which is unusual because Roger is exploring pain as musical inspiration.

The applause at the end of their set is enthusiastic rather than polite. This is a radical departure from their usual events, but the Bromley Arts Centre loves us and wants more.

I cannot remember exactly how many times we played in Bromley, but when the gigs ended several people had bought books on Tibetan Buddhism and I made a promise to myself to spend time at Samye Ling.

David kept his thoughts to himself. He probably knew that when the novelty wore off, most of us would only ever be dilettante Buddhists. One exception to this is Tony Visconti. He encountered Chime Rinpoche when I took him and Liz to meet Chime in Streatham. Tony has remained his student ever since.

I have never got around to asking Hanif Kureshi how he hit on the story line for his 1990 novel, *The Buddha of Suburbia*, which starts in Bromley in the 1970s and slowly moves to London. He changed it beyond all recognition, except for the David character, but it probably had some connection with our evenings in Bromley.

When BBC2 made a four-part drama series based on the book in 1993, David wrote the soundtrack for it, a mix of songs from the seventies and specially written numbers. The promotional music video for the series, featuring Bowie roaming suburban streets while singing the theme song, lives on on YouTube.

Myths and legends abound around that magical time in our lives and many a nostalgia session must have taken off into fantasy over the years. For me, Chime Rinpoche will always be the true Buddha of the south London suburbs.

While the Arts Lab, the Bromley gigs and The Three Tuns are in their heyday, Tony Visconti is working with David on his second album at Trident Studios in London. Tony likes everything David composes during this period – except for Space Oddity, which he regards as a superficial pop song.

Calvin Mark Lee, however, recognises its potential and finds someone else to take it on. That someone was the late Gus Dudgeon, who later found fame and fortune producing a number of high-profile entertainers, notably Elton John.

David tells me that Calvin sold some very collectable paintings by the artist Victor Vasarely in order to finance the recording of Space Oddity. He gives Gus Dudgeon *carte blanche* to hire the best available musicians and take as much studio time as he needs to turn Space Oddity into a hit single. Calvin's love for David and faith in his talent shines through his enigmatic Chinese-Californian personality.

I go with Angie to the final session, when they are putting the finishing touches to the recording. Hearing this song through studio speakers is mind-blowing for me. I heard it strummed in my kitchen, cobbled together at The Three Tuns and now here it is, transformed into state-of-the-art perfection by a maestro producer and top-notch musicians in one of the best recording studios in the world.

We all know it has to be a hit.

Crossing the chasm between recognition by the musical cognoscenti and being famous the way David Bowie is today is probably one of the most difficult, most elusive challenges in show business. Only a very small minority of very accomplished musicians make this transition – and many spend a lifetime trying.

With Space Oddity in the can and ready for release, David is on the cusp of a breakthrough – and I have an idea about how I can help him along.

For a couple of years I've been friends with John "Hoppy" Hopkins, co-founder and chief engineer of the underground newspaper *International Times* and a creative force behind the UFO club, the nursery of the Pink Floyd. I write occasional contributions for the paper but am careful not to overdo them, for fear of spooking the editors that give me paid work in the mainstream media.

Now known as *IT*, after a legal tiff with the owners of *The Times* and *Sunday Times*, it's a fearlessly anarchic, sexually explicit, politically abrasive, magnificent rag. It has a devoted countercultural following, stimulated by occasional splutters of righteous indignation from the *Daily Mail*, the Sunday *People* and other right-wing populist publications, as well as dismissive sneers from the left-wing *New Statesman*.

IT carries a music supplement, which has dramatically increased its circulation. I pitch an interview with David as a headline feature. It is gratefully accepted, so David and I spend a couple of evenings in conversation, which I record on what is probably one of the first portable open-reel tape machines.

The item appears as a double page spread on 15 August 1969. The stand-first copy, written by the editor of the music supplement, is a resume of David's pre-Space Oddity career.

The grammar is appalling but the history lesson is interesting.

> *David Bowie is, and always has been, one of those artists who seem to be on the periphery of pop; you can always sense their presence but you rarely see or hear them. Four years ago he was in fact touring the country in an improbably large van, which looked a bit like a racehorse transporter, with his band The Buzz, before that they were called Lower Third. He made several records, the best of which was Rubber Band b/w The Boys of London, but almost every dee jay that played the record likened his voice to that of Tony Newley and dismissed the record as that of a copyist. So Bowie went into seclusion for a while, became a solo performer with an acoustic guitar.*
>
> *Their (sic) followed a lot of chopping and changing, involvement with Buddhism, the formation of a mime troupe, all of which tended to fragment any effect he might*

have had on the pop world (yeuk!). Now he's trying for chart success again with his first record on Phillips (his previous ones were on Decca) entitled Space Oddity (see review on Sounds page) but this record is only one side to his career He is actively involved with Beckenham Arts Lab, which he started some months ago with journalist Mary Finnigan, who held the following interview with him.

Here is the entire interview as it appeared in *IT*.

MARY FINNIGAN: Tell me, where were you born?

DAVID BOWIE: Bromley.

MF: How old are you?

DB: 22

M: How long have you been in show-business?

D: Big blondes with blue eyes.

M: How do you like your cabbage cooked?

D: Fast cars and I shit regularly.

M: One of the first things that was said to me about you was: 'David's always had everything going for him.' Then I thought, 'How strange he hasn't got any money,' – but you do come over very positive, particularly when you think about this big ego trip about posterity and your song.

D: That's incredible – I want it to be the first anthem of the moon – play it as they hoist the flag and all that… 'For here am I sitting in a tin can, far above the world, the planet earth is blue and there's nothing I can do.'

Group 16: *Time, Out & Sounds, August 16-23, 1969.* • Plate 1(b)

an interview with

DAVID BOWIE

Interviewed by MARY FINNIGAN

DAVID BOWIE is, and has always been, one of those artists who seem to be on the periphery of pop; you can always sense their presence but you rarely see or hear them. Four years ago he was in fact touring the country in an improbably large van which looked a bit like a race horse transporter with his band, 'The Buzz', before that they were called 'Lower Third'. He made several records, the best of which was 'Rubber Band' b/w 'The Boys of London', but almost every dee-jay that played the record likened his voice to that of Tony Newley and dismissed the record as that of a copyist. So Bowie went into reclusion for a while, became a solo performer with acoustic guitar.

Then followed a lot of chopping and changing, involvement with Buddhism, the formation of a mime troupe, all of which tended to fragment any effect he might have had on the 'pop world' (yeah!). Now he's trying for chart success again with his first record on Phillips, (his previous ones were on Decca), entitled 'Space Oddity' (see review on 'Sounds Page') but this record is only one side to his career. He is actively involved with Beckenham Arts Lab, which he started some months ago with journalist Mary Finnigan, who held the following interview with him.

John
Bar
NEW
SINGLE

MF 119
[MERCURY]

MARY FINNIGAN: Tell me, where were you born?
DAVID BOWIE: Bromley.
MF: How old are you?
DB: 22
M: How long have you been in showbusiness?
D: Six years, with blue eyes.

Instead of authority structures, apart from just schooling instinct I had a piece of the weird aspects of it — here wanting authorities can be and that this is what so many, many people. I carried that through with me, well, as I said, I got dissatisfied with the group thing and had to get away from showbusiness completely. I got interested in Buddhism and had a big re-think about where I was at.

M: But it's not a 'Glory Hallelujah' song, you don't think in those terms.

D: No, it's downbeat. Major Tom, the hero – anti-hero if you like – is a loser and that has a huge sphere of identification in people's minds. There are so many losers and they all think that if they'd been in Frank Borman's place, for example, something would have certainly gone wrong.

M: I wonder if you will still live within the same social framework if the record goes to number one?

D: Yes, why not. We'll invite the straight journalists back to your flat after the Folk Club and Bowie will still be doing the same things and not answering the same questions. The people who are attracted by the charts will see an Arts Lab actually happening, because my relationship with my own scene won't change.

M: Are you sure of that?

D: Absolutely. Part of my motivation in doing a hit parade number is to promote the Arts Labs along with it, but without elitist attitudes. Arts Labs should be for everybody – not just the so-called turned-on minority... we need energy from all directions, heads and skin-heads alike.

M: When you made your first record, the very first time you set foot inside a recording studio as an artist, was the feeling in your head the same as it is now?

D: Yes it was. As far as aims and objectives are concerned I always wanted to promote things. It was very, very localised even then. If the record got into the charts I was thinking of the things I could do in Bromley. I seem to have come round in a circle, but changed course in the middle... here I am in Beckenham two years later with the same thought.

M: It seems to me that starting ripples in a concentrated area, then letting them spread outwards if they're going to, is very fundamental to your nature...

D: Yes, this happened before, it reached a peak then tailed off when I went to live in London. But also I got fed up with working with groups and I disappeared completely – submerged myself...

M: This was when you were thinking of retiring to a Buddhist monastery?

D: Yes, it was because I was dissatisfied with the things I was doing that I started thinking about Buddhism again and went through some very serious changes. At school I'd been interested in Buddhism and beatnik writing - it was beatnik in those days – I was in to people like Allen Ginsberg and Jack Kerouac when I was about 14 or 15. I'd already felt strongly about the the unfairness of authority structures, apart from just schoolboy instincts I had a grasp of the social aspects of it – how wrong authorities can be and that this is unfair on many, many people. I carried that through with me, until, as I said, I got dissatisfied with the group thing and had to get away from show-business completely. I got immersed in Buddhism and had a big re-think about where I was at.

M: Did this happen before or after your first LP?

D: After. The LP was behind me, it was the first thing I did as a solo artist again. It went solo, groups, solo, nothing, mime, group, duo, solo... you're up to date.

M: The last bit was a gradual re-emergence...

D: Yes, it was a most important transitional period. Mime doesn't need words, then I got into Feathers with Hermione and Hutch and we had music and movement. I started singing again, then coming out completely as a singer, doing exactly what I wanted to do in the beginning...

M: Back to square one...

D: The David Bowie career was a physical manifestation of where I was at spiritually – it may seem that I've moved around a lot, but at least I was honest to my head... 'The wild-eyed boy stumbled back to cry among the clouds, kicking back the pebbles from the freecloud mountain track.'

M: I think we've come upon a paradox now – for example if you were to play Space Oddity to two or three people hearing it for the first time and then play them the tape of this interview the two would bear no relation to each other – they would think, 'This man must be in an advanced state of schizophrenia...'

D. Yes.

M: Do you look upon Major Tom as an alter ego figure?

D: Well – we drew this parallel that the publicity image of a spaceman at work is of an automaton rather than a human being and my Major Tom is nothing if not a human being. It came from a feeling of sadness about this aspect of the space thing, it has been de-humanised, so I wrote a song-farce about it, to try and relate science and human emotion. I suppose it's an antidote to spacefever, really.

M: But it could also be a sign of the times - an indication of how thought produces a contrast to what is glaringly obvious...

D: It certainly doesn't lick Britannia's arse... imagine the 1990 version of 'All Our Yesterdays' with Space Oddity being used in the way they use 'Roll Out the Barrel' in documentaries about the First World War now – what a groove. I think schoolchildren ought to be taught songs like that, and other songs dealing with all kinds of businesses that they're likely to get into. Sort of nursery rhymes that show the other side of working in big stores or banks – songs about painful feet rather than fringe benefits and holidays with pay. Not in a revolutionary manner, just to point out the other side quite fairly. Although I'm right into the ideas and thought processes of the underground I don't really believe that the world is a place to be put right – Utopia is a mental state, not a physical one.

M: But this social realism thing has already been attempted – a lot of French singers do it very well.

D: In France yes, but there's very little like that in England. We're really a non-thinking race here, traditionalised and customised so much that we live by habit which is in-born, no thinking attached to it at all. It's just a set course of manners all the way.

M: We're very good at satire in this country, but that's not your line at all, is it?

D: No... I couldn't be that cruel really, I think it's unnecessary for me, but there are plenty of folk singers around who are satirists. A lot of them have a very sardonic approach, there's very little compassion around. I feel compassion as a source of energy, the individual is less important than the source of energy of which he is a part.

M: Is this the point at which you would admit a reverential attitude?

D: Yes. It's the totality and to cause pain would be as much of an injury to myself as it would be to others. It's a realisation of how important the totality is and how unimportant THIS all is!

M: This is a long way from Space Oddity, but I suppose there must be a thread somewhere?

D: Yes, there is a pattern running through it, because at the end of the song Major Tom is completely emotionless and expresses no view at all about where he's at... he gives up thinking completely...

M: But then Major Tom dissolves...

D: Exactly, he's fragmenting... at the end of the song his mind is completely blown – he's everything then.

M: D'you suppose when Paul Buckmaster was doing the arrangements for that song he had the same feelings about it as you?

D: Yeah.

M: Did you ever talk about it?

D: We've never talked about it, we just felt it. Paul looked at me, then he wrote down a few notes... then I looked at him and said, 'Yes, that's right...' But for all my years of education, I stand without a word to say...

M: You have this empathy with Paul – do you have it with Gus Dudgeon?

D: Yes I do but on a different plane completely. Gus is the technician, the arch 'mixer.' He listens to music and says, 'Yes, I like it – it's a groove,' his attitudes to music are very different from a lot of people in the business. With Tony Visconti, who's producing my LP, it's part of his life. He lives with music all day long, it's going on in his room, he writes it, arranges it, produces it, plays it, thinks it and believes very much in its spiritual source – his whole life is like this. One couldn't call him a conventional Buddhist, he's got a person religion, something he's gathered round him from all kinds of experience.

M: One supposes then that the single is the spearhead of your musical direction?

D: Yes, but at the same time it's an artistic entity in its own right. I'd like to make people aware that I want to spread my thoughts around. I'm not trying to educate people, or get them onto my way of thinking. It really doesn't bother me at all because the thinking thing is so stupid. It's incredibly hard to explain, strange but rather like a vast kind of personal brotherhood of everything...

M: You're into your totality again...

D: Yes I know, that's how it comes out all the time...

M: It's good, when I recognise it you know that you've made your point – to me anyway. But one of the criticisms I've heard of your songs is that you don't communicate to people who might not be tuned into the same vibrations.

D: Uuuuuuh – how can I say this? – I don't have to turn people on. If they are, then it's good, but if they're not then they're not. I feel that they will be turned on to a way of thinking which may be helpful to the human race and what's after it by just feeling the energy from my songs, if the energy has the right vibrations. It doesn't matter what the words say, the energy will be there.

M: Which is why I suppose that many of your thought processes and songs appear to be left suspended. I wonder if at some stage you might pick them up again.

D: Well no... it's like people learning to swim, you take them along something they know and can walk on right to the very end and then you bounce them off into the water. The springboard is something they know... then you just plunge 'em off into the energy at the end...

M: And there's a complete parallel with the way this whole commercial scene is set up, too, but on a much broader scale of course. These developments are happening as part of an overall plan you have in mind that you want to do three hit songs then retire from actually performing, which means that you hope to stretch your influence in different directions...

D: Yes, just into writing music, which is an extension of moving the energies. You get other people to do your songs, combining their energies with yours. One hopes that people believe in the songs they perform.

M: An interpretive addition?

D: Yes, it's little ripples going out in the beginning – then I drop bigger pebbles making harder ripples. I'm playing energy games... and I've got a vibration on this posterity thing, too. Following the pattern I've just mentioned I might help colour the waves that go into the future if Space Oddity goes to number one. I may help take away some of the veneer that would go through into the history books. I may show a little of the other side of what people were thinking... not just spacemen going up... and 'What kind of sandwiches are you eating?' or 'What shirts do you wear?' They weren't the only things people were thinking about...

M: I hate to draw comparisons, but there are several people one can quote as having been capable of projecting this and one of them is obviously Bob Dylan.

D: Yes, I really believe that Bob Dylan and others of the pop people have speeded up the changes. Without the communication level that they have created the things that have happened so far would still be ten years in the future... Prague,

Paris, London. Those things wouldn't have happened YET, I feel, without Dylan and the Beatles. These reports of war in the newspapers would just have been reports of war in the newspapers, but pop people put such an emphasis on the horror and futility of it all... pacifism has found a voice at last, and this voice is being heeded.

M: If you repeat anything loud enough to enough people for a long enough time it eventually gets through...

D: It's a conditioning, but I'm sure it's a conditioning in the right direction.

M: Getting back to this, if Space Oddity is a success d'you suppose we'll get inundated with sycophants at the folk club?

D: Not the folk people, they'll dig it but they won't push themselves forward. I wouldn't go rushing off to see Roy Harper if he had a club and found himself with a chart record. I suppose we'll get some like that, but not many.

M: That's good, but you can't ignore your actual everyday life when everybody wants to know you when you're a success but nobody cares a shit when you're not...

D: Yes, I suppose that applies to the pop scene, but it's not my world at all. The pop underground wouldn't come rushing at us. It's very good in its ideas and the way it sees things – so different to the pop establishment. If you want a comparison try putting our Arts Lab and the conventional theatre side by side and see what you get. Here we are in Beckenham with a

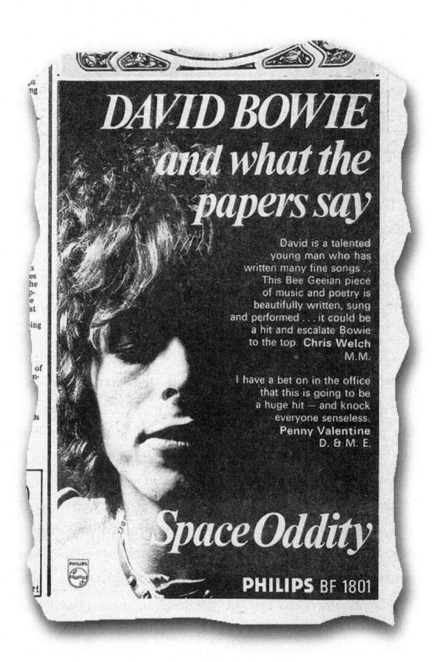

Ad in IT, August 1969

group of people creating their own momentum without the slightest concern for attitudes, tradition or pre-ordained moralities… it's alive, healthy and new and it matters to me more than anything else.

…

There is an uncomfortable irony involved in re-reading this interview, in the light of subsequent developments.

For example: "I wonder if you will still live within the same social framework if the record goes to number one?"

David: "Yes, why not? We'll invite the straight journalists back to your flat after the Folk Club and Bowie will still be doing the same things and not answering the same questions… my relationship with my own scene won't change."

David, did you really say that? Yes you did, because it is immortalised in print. More significantly, did you mean it?

Perhaps you meant it as you spoke into my tape recorder, but you certainly didn't mean it for some time before you left Beckenham. Your commitment to The Arts Lab and the egalitarian principles enshrined in its manifesto are quoted in other media, so you didn't utter those words just to please me. I should steer clear of speculation on what fuelled your change of heart and direction, but I suspect the combined influence of Angie and Tony Defries had something to do with it.

The *IT* interview may be the longest, most candid and thoughtful that David has ever done. He is unashamedly arty-intellectual (some might say high-falutin') – and also prophetic. He stresses that Space Oddity is about failure and Major Tom as a human being rather than an automaton – he sees it as a counterpoint to the propaganda surrounding the Space Race.

The essential nature of the song appears to be lost on the BBC. When they do their live broadcast of the first moon landing in July 1969 and the moment when Neil Armstrong makes history, they choose Space Oddity as the theme music.

About thirty Arts Lab enthusiasts gather in Foxgrove Road for this occasion, clustered around my small monochrome TV. David is not there, but Angie is up front – and inevitably throws a monster freak-out. It takes the combined efforts of the ever-present, ever-loving Spud and one or two others plus a hit of strong liquor to calm her down.

Party time at Foxgrove Road with Mick Ronson (left), David, Angie and Caroline's giant panda

David on the bandstand with fellow musicians at the 1969 Free Festival

THE FREE FESTIVAL

I wish I could remember how, where and when the idea for the Free Festival came into being. Sadly, the precise moment is lost in the dusty vaults of my memory bank. But I do recall that it gathered momentum at a phenomenal rate – around the time when The Three Tuns Sundays were peaking.

I was running like a gazelle with a lion on its tail, organising the festival, various Arts Lab projects, keeping house, doing *Sunday Times* shifts – and trying to snag an American folkie called Amory Kane, who played at the Tuns a couple of times. He epitomised tall, dark and handsome. He moved like a panther, sang about love and smiled like an angel. I'd recovered from being jilted and it was time to move on.

Painfully awkward about making the first moves, I created an illustrated storyboard to give him the message. He appeared to be flattered, but non-committal. He didn't explain why at the time. Years later he confessed that he hated himself for brushing me off and that it happened because he was going through terrible traumas with his wife.

July 1969. The mystique surrounding the Beckenham Arts Lab reaches central London and a steady flow of high-profile entertainers turn up to perform. Among them are rock stars Peter Frampton and Rick Wakeman, the folkie Bridget St John and the very famous writer and composer Lionel Bart. He does a half-hour monologue at The Three Tuns that earns him a standing ovation from our usual packed house that now spills out every week into the conservatory and garden.

The conservatory has turned into an arts and crafts market run by Chas and Liz. It does steady business, especially with sales of psychedelic posters. Lionel has an ulterior motive for making the trek to Beckenham. It is soon obvious that he has the hots for David.

Lionel turns up at Foxgrove Road in a white drop-head Rolls Royce. He is totally charming but makes it plain that my presence is not entirely welcome. After some hints, which I choose to ignore, he tosses the keys to the Roller at me and invites me to go away and play. It is an irresistible offer, so I spend the afternoon cruising around the neighbourhood – revelling in the thrill of driving a Rolls Royce.

I am not known for tact and discretion, but on this occasion I refrain from asking about what happened during my absence. Angie is nowhere to be seen that afternoon. It crosses my mind that David may have told her to vanish for a while – for a young performer trying to make his mark in show business, the patronage of an established star is very useful.

The excitement generated by our plans for the Free Festival infects everything we do. On Sunday nights in a warm July the proceedings at The Three Tuns accelerate into electrifying heights of creativity and inspiration. The music is super-charged, with feedback between audience and performers cranking up the buzz. There are moments when it feels more like a unified field, when the boundaries between audience and performance dissolve in a sensation that is close to the bliss experienced by yogis and mystics. The back room is packed tight – shoulder to shoulder, knee to knee and hand to hand.

Chas is lord of the conservatory marketplace, where the artists and artisans of south London sell their wares. In the garden, members of the London musical elite toke on their reefers and prowl, with eyes and ears open to the opportunities that might arise from this latest happening scene.

Space Oddity is getting air play on pop radio – and that makes previously snooty movers and shakers less blasé about the suburbs. It looks increasingly likely that Space Oddity will make the charts, which forces them to take notice.

My friend the late John "Hoppy" Hopkins was a pioneer by nature. When he tired of photography, *IT* held his attention for a while, but then it shifted to the technological leading edge. He founded BIT Information Service – and soon afterwards discovered that the techno giant Sony was marketing a portable video recorder. Hoppy spotted its potential, acquired a couple of Sony Portapacks and started out on a new career in video reportage.

The moment I hear about Hoppy's latest enthusiasm I invite him to Beckenham to record at The Three Tuns. Hoppy has finely tuned antennae for emerging trends but in this instance they desert him. He turns down the invitation and, in so doing, misses the opportunity to video the launch pad of

David Bowie's career – and to create a record of the community spirit that prevails during that time.

Everyone connected with Growth is involved for idealistic reasons. We see ourselves as a model for a new society rooted in love, altruism and humanitarian values. I have to take it on trust that David is sincere about this, though subsequent events leave me in doubt.

Meanwhile, manager Ken Pitt is still trying to promote David as a version of mainstream pop icons like Tommy Steele or Cliff Richard. With this in mind, he sets up appearances for David at song festivals in Malta and Italy. His timing could not have been worse. David feels obliged to go along with it, but it takes him away during the most intense period prior to the Free Festival.

I am left to pull the strings and press the levers to make it happen – with a workforce that consists of enthusiastic but largely uncontrollable hippies, most of whom are still supported by their parents, have never had a job and are barely out of their teens.

There is manic activity at Foxgrove Road as 16 August, the date for the Free Festival, approaches. We are scornful of bureaucracy but learn late in the preparations that we need a permit to stage an event at the Croydon Road Recreation Ground. This is essential because we need electricity at the bandstand where we are putting on amplified music. We make a mad dash to Bromley to do the paperwork, pay a fiver and we are official. It is all astonishingly cheap and easy.

I attempt to co-ordinate the various strands, with help from Angie and assorted Arts Lab devotees, but the pre-festival planning is continuously on the verge of chaos, and I spend my days dealing with it as best I can. Right up to the last twenty-four hours I have no idea how many people will turn up with attractions like food and drink stalls, arts and crafts and other forms of entertainment apart from music.

David is supposed to be in charge of the music and before he leaves he does invite lots of artists to take part. We don't know who or how many will turn up. Some of them are coming from London, but many are local, very young and inexperienced. They needed help with things like transport, equipment and timing. "What time am I on?" is the most frequently asked question. I cannot not answer it. "Just turn up, hang out by the bandstand and I'm sure David will tell you when to do your thing" is the best advice I can offer.

Angie rolls up her sleeves and gets behind the operation. In fact, I have to admit that I probably wouldn't be able to manage without her. Between us we try to keep tabs on who is doing what – drinks stand, candy floss, sandwiches, puppet theatre, face-painting and so on.

Angie organises her own contribution – a wheelbarrow barbecue that is hugely popular on the day. She makes sure Calvin Mark Lee is teed up to bring San Francisco psychedelic rock posters for sale. It is a Free Festival modelled on Wood-stock in the USA and probably the first of its kind in the UK, but we are hoping to make money which might enable the Arts Lab to rent premises.

The psychedelic jungle drums send the message far and wide. Bob Harris gives the festival a plug in the recently launched *Time Out*. His friend Tim Goffe volunteers to DJ between acts. I write a piece for *IT* and the local newspapers give us mentions. We have no idea how many people will come, but our expectations are high.

At one point David's dad, Haywood Jones, phones to speak to his son and I have to tell him David is in Italy. Mr. Jones sounds croaky but gives no indication that he is seriously ill. I neglect Caroline and Richard – but thankfully Peter Finnigan takes them off on holiday and I no longer have to rely on Spud and feel guilty.

On Sunday 3 August David comes back from Italy triumphant – a few days before the Free Festival. He has won first prize at the Carosello Internaziale del Disco for Best Produced Record for his performance of "When I Live My Dream" – and he has a statuette to prove it.

I don't manage to talk to him before The Three Tuns, so I have to shout the news over the hubbub that his dad phoned and didn't sound too good. Extremely angry because he has not been told earlier, David flounces out of the pub to call his father.

Mr. Jones has been taken to hospital with pneumonia and dies two days later.

This is a terrible blow for David. He is distraught and so is his mother. Angie and David decamp to the family home in Bromley in order to support his mum – and I am left to deal with preparations for a festival that is less than a week away from lift-off. But even in the face of sudden death, the show must go on.

David's mood is dark, depressed and surly, but he does his share of the last-minute adjustments. It is not easy for any of us – he snaps and snarls his way through what needs to be accomplished, especially at me because he had not forgiven me for waiting to tell him about his Dad's phone call. This was the way he sees it, but it is not fair, because I did tell him at the first available opportunity.

Saturday 16 August 1969 dawns with clear blue skies and sparkling sunshine. Angie has stayed at Foxgrove Road overnight so she could load her barbecue kit (including large wheelbarrow), buns, burgers, paper plates, ketchup etc. into Suzy's van when it shows up. David is coming from Bromley. He's organised transport for the stage gear, which has already left the flat.

Angie is not her usual glamorous self. Dressed for a messy afternoon, she wears David's old red cord jeans and a flimsy blouse that she knots under her boobs. In contrast, my outfit is the epitome of hippy chic. Spray-on purple bell bottoms, skinny yellow top, a beaded hipster belt and oversize shades. I have long, thick glossy hair and a body that curves in all the right places. I go heavy on the eye makeup.

I know I look OK but I'm a bundle of nerves as we wait for Suzy. Eventually she turns up, a little breathless and beaming her usual big smile and steady vibes. Instantly calming when others have the jitters, Suzy is a treasure beyond price.

We can hear the PA system tests in progress while some distance away from the Recreation Ground. It is a large sprawling park with ponds, play zones, dense patches of bushes and trees and as its central focus, a spacious area of grass around a fine Victorian wrought-iron bandstand. This is the festival arena.

As I arrive, there is activity in all directions. The Arts Lab people, who David and I had cajoled, nurtured and occasionally cursed, come up trumps, with enough controlled energy to turn the idea we floated during stoned conversation into the reality of that day.

I don't have to do very much except stroll around admiring the stalls and installations taking shape in the morning sunshine. Everyone is happy (except for David) and the scene is set for an outstandingly wonder-full day. Thankfully, the overall positive energy and enthusiasm triumph over David's black mood. He alone is sulky, irritable and monosyllabic. When he speaks, it is either to snarl at someone for a perceived error or to bark an order to the guys setting up the stage.

We understand the effects of unexpected loss of a beloved parent and steer clear of him as much as possible.

Calvin arrives with a big pile of original Californian psychedelic posters, which are already collectors' items. To my astonishment and delight, he donates them for sale, rather than
asking for a 50-50 split. David fails to appreciate the generosity
of this gesture and is as rude to Calvin as he is to the rest of us.
With his customary West Coast cool Calvin shrugs, while I
cringe and help him set up his pitch.

On stage at the Free Festival

This is not a book about David Bowie's songs. There are lots already written. It is a book about a unique slice of history, when the young people of south London were united in a magical experience that peaked on the afternoon of 16 August. I can write reasonable prose, but I am not a genius poet and musician. David Bowie is of that calibre. The words of his song "Memory of a Free Festival" and the melody that goes with them reflect the atmosphere of that day better than any attempt I can make to do the same.

If you are wondering why the lyrics are not quoted here, the answer is they were – until the eagle-eyed author and journalist Wendy Leigh pointed out that the "fair use" convention around copyrighted material applies in the United States, but not in the UK or many other countries worldwide. I suggested that David would not sue if we kept them in. Wendy responded, "It's not him, it's the people around him." And of course she is right. The music business is ferociously financial – Mammon (god of wealth) trumps Saraswati (goddess of knowledge, music, arts, wisdom and learning.) every time.

David's song compares the ecstasy of that afternoon to the state of *satori* - the union of bliss and emptiness in Buddhist meditation. For many of us who were lucky enough to be there, this is the abiding memory of Britain's first free festival, which happened in the south London suburb of Beckenham, replicating the spirit of the one that preceded it in Woodstock, USA. More free festivals came later, including Windsor, which ran for a few years and was then trounced by an indignant establishment, and Stonehenge, which ended after the infamous Battle of the Beanfield. Such anarchy – people having fun on their own terms, with cash flow as a by-product rather than a prerequisite – provoked deep unease within the UK's dominant elite, just as it does in the post-millennium environment.

There are no ticket sales for free festivals, so it is impossible to say how many people contribute to the Beckenham ecstasy, but it must be at least a thousand and probably more.

It is a perfect day in every respect. David the professional entertainer gives no hint of the pain he carries to the crowd that come to hear the music and be refreshed and renewed by the shared experience of the festival spirit.

Pretty well every musician who played at the Three Tuns turns up for the festival. The Strawbs, Keith Christmas, Gun Hill, Amory Kane, Tony Visconti, Comus, Bridget St John and a very sexy flute player called Mox – plus a local band called Appendix To Part 1, led by 16-year-old Bill Liesegang. John Peel was supposed to be with us but does a no show. Luckily my friend Jo's brother, Tim Goffe, turns up to DJ between acts. I lose count of how many times he plays Space Oddity.

David's song touches on marijuana as part of the mix that generated the bliss. It was totally open and relaxed – reefers are rolled and smoked as PC Sam Wheller in uniform strolls in our midst. He parks his sense of smell for the day and smiles benevolently. I think he gets a contact high.

Mary and Angie at the Free Festival 1969;
Angie grilling on her wheelbarrow barbecue.

David claims to have kissed a lot of people that day. It is such a pity this is not true. In his grief he was unapproachable and definitely not kissable. But the most surprising and delightful *denouement* to that unforgettable afternoon is that he recreated it in a song, which became an anthem celebrating the best of the 1960s, even though he did not experience the full measure of it.

Time becomes supersonic when you are having so much fun. All too soon the sun sinks behind the trees and there is a gradual exodus as people pack up and leave. Angie could have sold twice as many burgers.

Dave Walkling recalls his role as Angie's assistant: "She did the cooking, I handed out the burgers and took the money. At the end of the day we made £30 – an ecstatic moment! Angie picked me up and whirled me round in a giant bear hug."

Calvin sells all his posters, Chas and Liz run out of candy floss. Every Arts Lab person who had things to sell brings the proceeds to me. I stand by the exit with a bag full of money. When it really is all over, several of us pile into a car and drive back to Foxgrove Road.

We tip the cash onto my bed and count it. The mood is jubilant – we have curated a free festival, given pleasure to lots of people and had a fabulous day ourselves. And to top it all we make a £200 profit – equivalent to more than £3,000 in 2016 money. Suddenly there is a thundercloud in the doorway.

"You make me sick," growls David. "You're just a bunch of bread-heads – you don't care about anything except money." Then he stomps out. The outburst has a sobering effect. We gather the cash and disperse. A sour end to a very sweet day.

I cannot remember who took charge of the money and I never saw it again. It was probably Chas Lippeatt, because he later became the cheerleader who kept the Arts Lab afloat for a while – and found it a home in a shed by the railway line in Penge.

Nick Jennings was one of the few Growth enthusiasts who did not come to the Free Festival. He was inner circle with David, Angie and me, appreciated for his wit and intelligence. He shared an interest in Tibetan Buddhism and chose to go to Samye Ling rather than Croydon Road Recreation Ground.

With DJ Tim Goffe

SAMYE LING AND BEYOND

After the intensity of the previous months I am physically and emotionally exhausted. I've packed in more experience during this period than at any other time in my life. It's been a steep and rewarding learning curve – but I need a rest.

Peter Finnigan takes care of Caroline and Richard and I catch the overnight train to Scotland to join Nick at the first Tibetan Buddhist institution in the developed world.

A cheerful bloke called Jock meets me at Lockerbie station. As we drive through the low Dumfriesshire hills, I have a strong sensation that this is the start of a new phase, that I will finally get serious about meditation.

It turns out to be a false start, because Akong Rinpoche, the founder and head honcho at Samye Ling is away on a visit to Tibet – and the centre is functioning more like a rest home for burned-out hippies than a Buddhist retreat.

As we swing into the driveway, the only evidence I see of a Tibetan presence are some prayer flags hanging between two trees. The sign on the gate says Johnstone House. Jock deposits me at the doorway to a dilapidated Victorian hunting lodge that has seen better days. Someone has painted the exterior woodwork in the primary colours beloved by Tibetans, but apart from that it looks like it would benefit from a comprehensive makeover.

Akong has left his younger brother Jamdra in charge of the centre. Jamdra has Jimi Hendrix hair, slouches around in velvet bell-bottoms and an Afghan coat and is thoroughly bored and miserable. Samye Ling is the last place Jamdra wants to be. He was there because big brother has pulled rank, but Jamdra is yearning to get back to sex 'n' drugs 'n' rock 'n' roll in London.

He later had a Road to Damascus experience, abandoned hedonism, was ordained a monk and is known as Lama Yeshe Losal – in charge of Samye Ling and its various offshoots, including a retreat centre on Holy Island. In 2011 Akong Rinpoche was murdered by a disgruntled young Tibetan while on a visit to one of his charitable projects in eastern Tibet, an area now annexed as part of China.

Nick detaches himself from a group of bright young things lounging on a ha-ha wall and floats towards me in a Gandalf cape.

"Great, you made it," he says with a Cheshire cat grin. "Follow me."

Nick gives me a tour guide introduction to the delights of Samye Ling. The shrine room is complete with ornate altar, giant Buddha statue and thangka paintings depicting serene Tantric deities, alongside fearsome creatures with bloody fangs dancing on dead bodies in a halo of flames. I love it on sight.

We visit the vegetable garden and say hello to Elizabeth the gardener who lives in a greenhouse.

We go to the River Esk which flows through the Samye Ling land, where Nick shows me a rock where you can sit in the middle of the river and chant mantras in harmony with the roaring water all around. Then we cross the road and climb a wooded hill on the other side, where a secret altar has evolved – more shamanic, earthier, more connected with *spiritus localis*.

Nick delves into a pocket and hands me a capsule. "Mescaline," he says. "Fancy a trip tomorrow?" I certainly do, and for the time being put aside my aspiration to give up drugs and take up meditation.

I stay for two weeks at Samye Ling and eventually find an American who teaches me basic breath-awareness meditation. It feels entirely natural to get up before dawn and shuffle into the shrine room, to sit for an hour with a small group of people, cross-legged, straight-backed and silent beneath blanket-shrouded shoulders.

This encounter establishes a pattern which has endured for the rest of my life. I don't get up so early now, but am forever thankful for the karmic pathway which led me into Tibetan Buddhism.

I thought a lot at Samye Ling about the karma that came to fruition with the opportunity to live and work with David Bowie, to found the Beckenham Arts Lab with him and to experience that summer of love, anarchy and social cohesion.

At Haddon Hall

Yes, I know there's an apparent contradiction here, but that's the paradox of life as we know it, and anarchy doesn't mean chaos. I reflected on everything that happened and realised that I had neglected my children and my profession in favour of those few short months of novelty and excitement. It was time to recalibrate and to reclaim my flat as a family home.

David and Angie are staying at Foxgrove Road while I am away, thinking along similar lines. Space Oddity has climbed the charts, although it fails to make number one. Its success means that at last there is money flowing into the Bowie coffers – not a lot, but enough to finance a rented apartment. They really do need their own living space.

Angie, forever the practical fixer, goes flat-hunting and eventually finds a suitably romantic one available for rent in an Edwardian Gothic mansion a few minutes' walk away on Southend Road. The house is called Haddon Hall. Angie negotiates the ground-floor flat for a modest rent of £7 per week. Tony Visconti and his girlfriend Liz agree to share it with them.

The flat is rather grand and imposing, with obvious rock star potential. It has a huge hallway with a minstrel's gallery above it, set against a floor-to-ceiling stained glass window. Three large rooms open off the hall, plus a tiny kitchen and even tinier bathroom. With very limited funds, Angie the domestic goddess sets about making it comfortable.

Meanwhile The Three Tuns still happens every Sunday, with David and Angie participating. Barry and Christina have bowed out, there are no lightshow projectors and it has pretty well turned into a standard folk night – with some amplified rock thrown in.

The atmosphere has lost its electrical charge. People who come seem to want to be passively entertained, rather than participating in an inclusive experience. It is anti-climactic. David picks up on this and says so. After a while he gives up on the folk nights, which are taken over by a guy called Ken Simmons.

The collective ethos of the Arts Lab starts to fall apart as well. It becomes obvious that David and I had fulfilled leadership roles, although we never intended to do so. With us no longer holding the centre ground, petty power struggles develop – which send both of us running for the hills.

I get my flat and my life back, but it feels rather empty and I drift again, waiting for what astrologers would probably describe as a planetary shift.

Growth potters on for a while. I never go to the hut by the railway line but hear about it from time to time. I gather it is mostly a print workshop and that Brian Moore and his puppet theatre use it as well. Sometime later I hear that it has run out of energy and has closed down – which brings a great adventure to an end with a whimper.

Around Christmas 1969 a London friend called Carolyn Brown comes to stay at Foxgrove Road. She presents me with a proposition that is extremely enticing but also a big challenge for me.

Carolyn is an American from California and a graduate of the Haight-Ashbury drug culture. We have considerable psychedelic experience in common and also, it turns out, a desire to move on into a contemplative tradition that does not involve plant or chemical catalysts. Carolyn is interested in Tibetan Buddhism. So am I. Carolyn says the best place to go to find a Tibetan guru is India. She asks if I would like to travel with her.

"Like" is not the operative word. Of course I would love to go to India, and street-wise Carolyn seems to be an ideal travel companion. But I have two children and they need their mother. Or do they? I agonise over this dilemma for some time – until Carolyn becomes impatient and says she'll look for someone else to go with her if I can't make up my mind.

The planetary shift occurs soon afterwards, when a couple with a child of their own arrive on the doorstep, asking if I know of a place where they can live for a few months. They are friends of David and Angie and seem like reliable, kind people. I suggest a proposition to them – live in my flat for free for six months and look after my children while I'm away. They agree and I start planning my new adventure.

Number one priority is to do it on the cheap. Both of us have very limited funds so we end up booking ourselves onto a flight to Bombay (Mumbai) with a Yemeni airline in an ancient piston engine aircraft. We take off on a cold January morning.

Our first stop is Cairo and as the plane circles waiting to land we are treated to a bird's eye view of the pyramids. The UK's grey skies and drizzle are replaced by bright sunshine. Our second stop is Aden. When we return to the aircraft it has been loaded up with big wooden crates that block all but squeeze space between the seats and the loo. This was extremely dodgy and probably against a slew of aviation regulations – even in 1970. But in our excitement at the start of a leap into the unknown, we are in no mood to quibble.

We spend two days in a very cheap hotel in Bombay which has the advantage of a dope seller and his family living on the staircase. This enables us to score a nice lump of legendary Bombay Black charas to take with us to Goa. We were told by friends in London that the best way to ease oneself into India is to spend some time on Calangute beach in Goa. This turns out to be excellent advice.

In those days a passenger steamer left Bombay every day at nightfall, ploughed down the Konkani coast and docked at Goa the following morning. The night is warm, the stars are incandescent and a half moon hangs in the sky. The sea is calm. We stretch out on slatted wooden seats on deck and sigh with contentment.

Sometime later a young man appears. He has mid-length hair, a scraggy beard and a dark tan. He's wearing thong sandals, baggy once-white cotton trousers and a mirrored waistcoat.

"Hello," he says. "I'm Ben. You look like you've just got off a plane from Europe."

Ben hunkers down beside us, rolls a spliff with our Bombay Black and, as the stone takes off, launches into a monologue of useful information for India novices. He tells us where to go in Goa, who to seek out, who and what to avoid. He tells us about the Catholic priest who is also black market money changer and accommodation Mr. Fixit. We discover mutual acquaintances both in India and London. Ben has been a hip traveller for several years, has no intention of returning home in the foreseeable future and seems happy, healthy and wise. We learn that he had a well-paid job for several years and is now living on his savings.

"Hard currency goes a long way in India if you are careful," he says.

As the conversation tails off, we space out into a state of bliss. The tensions involved in preparing for the trip and the long-distance travel into an alien culture dissolve as the boat chugs gently across a calm sea, a gazillion stars twinkle and a half moon hangs from an indigo sky. We say goodbye to Ben when we disembark in Goa and never see him again. As our journey progresses we learn that passing on travel tips to fellow pilgrims is integral to the hip/backpacker culture. Ben turns out to be the first of many bodhisattvas of this ilk, and we in turn contribute to the oral transmission.

Carolyn and I find a nice house on Baga beach in Goa recently vacated by our friend Andy Miller Mundy. We stay for six weeks and have a totally delightful time, doing very little except eating, sleeping, socialising and taking drugs. There are lots of western hippies living on the beach between Baga and Calangute and we get to know many of them. As the sun goes down, most evenings we sit on our veranda preparing food. People drift in to join us, and then we move on together to another house where, for example, a new friend is preparing opium tea.

This involves filtering raw opium several times after boiling it up with syrup and spices. It turns out to be a very potent concoction which sends me off into a warm, extremely seductive stoned embrace for several hours. One has to be careful because there's just about every psychoactive drug in contemporary use freely available on Baga beach. There are heavy users of very heavy dope around – some of whom appear to be in the process of committing slow suicide.

It is a simple life, with two- or three-room fisher-folk houses spaced widely apart, no electricity, no running water, no bathrooms. Sanitation comes in the form of narrow wooden huts with a platform inside with a hole in the middle. These are notorious because when you dump, one of the local free-roaming pigs is instantly there beneath the hole, gobbling up your offering before you have time to stand up. This puts most of us off eating pork.

Today Baga beach has disappeared under several miles of concrete. It has been subsumed into the mass tourism circuit and resembles one of the less salubrious Spanish Costa resorts. The hippies are long gone, but small enclaves hang on around southern Goa, Anjuna and Vagator to the north.

We travel third class on a train pulled by an ancient steam engine from Bombay to Varanasi. A 24-hour nightmare journey. I vow never to do anything like it again. But once installed in the Tourist Bungalow in India's great holy city our luck returns. Two Indian businessmen offer us tickets to hear the late, great sitar maestro Ravi Shankar. We spend a magical night at an open-air restaurant, listening to him playing to a predominantly Indian audience on his home territory – an experience that is etched forever into my DNA. It laid the foundations for my later appreciation of world music.

We ride with several other travellers in a VW van from Varanasi to Kathmandu – a trip that takes the best part of three days across the plains to Patna before gradually climbing into the mind-blowing beauty of the Himalayan foothills.

We start out well in Kathmandu, meeting up with friends from London and hanging out around the exquisitely carved pagoda temples that suffered such tragic damage in the 2015 earthquakes. We drop acid on full moon night in Swayambhu, close to the magnificent stupa, together with at least a hundred similarly intoxicated westerners. We smoke chillums at dawn to prolong the magic. In 1970 cannabis was legal in Nepal, but the Nepalese government caved in to pressure from the USA a couple of years later and instigated prohibition, torpedoing the economic potential of their most lucrative natural resource.

We had shedloads of fun in Goa and Kathmandu, but that is not the intention of our trip. The hip travellers are predominantly dilettante Buddhists. They wear malas, dorjes and other ritual paraphernalia as fashion accessories. They chant "Om Ah Hung" as a form of tribal identification. They are not into study and practice as serious neophytes.

Carolyn and I have been through the psychedelic experience, we have immersed ourselves in the delicious hedonism of sex 'n' drugs 'n' rock 'n' roll. Now we wanted to find out if it was leading us into another deeper, more challenging and less physically and mentally dangerous arena. We were eager to learn and keen to find experts to teach us.

Even in Nepal we soon discover that in 1970 English-speaking, accomplished Tibetan lamas are very thin on the ground. After asking around for several days, we are eventually directed to a woman known as "the Russian princess." It transpires that she lives on Kopan hill, above the Boudnath stupa a few miles from the city centre.

We take a bus to Bouda, pay our respects to the great stupa and after asking directions set off through an idyllic rural landscape to Kopan.

The Russian-American woman turns out to be a nun rather than a princess. Her name is Zina Rachevsky. We have picked up rumours about her colourful life story – most of which turn out to be true. A former international socialite, fashion model, film starlet and showgirl, Zina is a raving beauty who had a Road-to-Damascus experience, renounced her attachment to the material world and was ordained as a Tibetan Buddhist nun in the Gelugpa tradition by Trijang Rinpoche, the Dalai Lama's senior tutor.

Zina's mission in her new life is to become a contemplative yogini – and to create an environment where other westerners can study and practice Tibetan Buddhism. Kopan is in its infancy as a meditation centre, but to our delight there are two very interesting lamas there – Thubten Yeshe and his disciple, Thubten Zopa Rinpoche. Zopa speaks enough English to make the subtleties of Vajrayana Buddhist theory and basic practice accessible to the small group of westerners resident on Kopan hill, a rural refuge with breathtaking views over the Kathmandu valley and the mighty Himalayan ranges beyond. Lama Yeshe is a unique and wonderfully eccentric personality. What he lacks in English vocabulary he makes up for ten times over in wisdom and warmth.

We have a brief encounter with Zina and she agrees to let us stay at her house until we find a place of our own. Then she vanishes into retreat. We live for nine weeks on Kopan hill in a thatched wattle and daub farmhouse and I have to say it is one of the happiest periods of my life. I spend days alone on the hilltop, gazing at the mountains, chanting my newly acquired mantra, meditating silently and dozing off in my sleeping bag under the moon and stars.

This was the start of my ongoing commitment to Tibetan Buddhist practice, and I have to thank David Bowie for the initial introduction. In Nepal I was not at all sure about what I was doing and why I was attracted to the lamas. It was not until several years later that I had what could be described as a contemplative breakthrough.

After a while at Kopan it becomes clear that Carolyn and I will have to reach a parting of the ways. As the monsoon rains come tumbling down for days at a stretch, I find living in a primitive farmhouse too much to deal with. I've been away for nearly six months and am ready to go home. Carolyn wants to stay and carry on taking teachings from the two Thubtens.

HOMECOMING

We flew to Bombay on one-way tickets – now I have to find my way back to the UK overland alone and on very little money. I travel by bus with friends from Delhi to Kabul via Rawalpindi, Peshawar and the Khyber Pass. I hop a plane from Kabul to Tehran and then more bus rides to Istanbul. Stuck there with money almost gone, I hate the place and the continuous sex hassles from pretty well every man I encounter.

Eventually I spend my last cash on a bus ride to Munich via Bulgaria and the former Yugoslavia. There's only one driver and during our second night on the road he is pretty well asleep at the wheel. We end up stationary behind another bus, straddling a railway line with a train approaching. Thankfully a quick witted passenger shakes our driver awake and he hits reverse gear a second or two before the train roars past the front end of the bus.

I run out of money in Munich, but do a deal with an American couple who pay my fare to London in return for a place to stay for a while at Foxgrove Road. Peter Finnigan is on the quayside in Dover with Caroline and Richard. We have an emotional reunion. Things did not work out too well with the people who were supposed to look after the children and Peter had to step in to the rescue. I am not top of the family popularity ratings.

I do, however, get a warm welcome from David and Angie, who are by now enjoying cosy domesticity at Haddon Hall. Over delicious dinners cooked by Angie, they update me on events in their lives. During my absence Space Oddity has progressed from a hit single into a space-age anthem. David's eponymous second album is released to critical acclaim. It consists mostly of material written while he was at Foxgrove Road and is elegantly produced by Tony Visconti. The last track is "Memory of a Free Festival." It brings tears to my eyes when I hear it for the first time.

They tell me that this raised David's profile with the showbiz moguls – briefly – and that he wrote and recorded more singles with chart potential, especially "The Prettiest Star," which should have struck gold but, despite some airplay, sank without trace.

Somewhere along this timeline David and Angie got married. They show me photos of the wedding at Bromley Register Office with both of them still looking hippyish. But Angie's hair is now shorter – and David's a lot longer – and they are increasingly androgynous.

At a party at Foxgrove Road they are lying on the floor side by side, face down in front of the fireplace. Tony Visconti remarks that it is difficult to tell them apart. I am delighted that our friendship survives the absences, upheavals and changing dynamics of our lives.

Angie and Liz do not see eye to eye on domestic arrangements and eventually Tony and Liz move out of the flat at Haddon Hall. They are replaced by assorted musicians who mostly crash in the minstrels' gallery.

The place morphs into a musical commune for a while and during this period David writes and releases two more albums. The loud, sombre *The Man Who Sold The World* and, after the birth of his son Zowie (now Duncan), the cheerful, melodic *Hunky Dory*, which is my favourite Bowie album. Neither of them make much of an impact.

Angie is miserable during her pregnancy. Having a bulging tummy and fulfilling a feminine role does not resonate with her essential nature. Angie is fundamentally bisexual, while I am beginning to realise that David plays being bi as a theatrical role, because it chimes with the emerging pop zeitgeist. It suits his purpose rather than his instincts.

I am home alone one evening after returning from India, when there is an unexpected knock on the door. It is a heavily pregnant Angie looking distraught. "Hello Finns," she says. "Can I come in?"

I make tea and offer sympathy but she will not open up to why she is distressed. I suspect she's done a runner after a row with David. She sits glumly beside me for an hour or so, then, as fast as she arrived, she's gone. I feel sorry for her because in essence I like Angie. She's as batty as Dracula's cave, but her heart is sound and her intentions are usually directed at being nice to people.

I suffer a full blast of culture shock after six months in India. Angie was understanding and supportive while I was discombobulated. I feel helpless now because she will not allow me to reciprocate.

Whatever magic we conjured up with the Arts Lab apparently had a magnetic effect on working musicians. One day I spot one of the high priests of the psychedelic era shopping in Beckenham High Street. It turns out that Arthur Brown and members of his band, Kingdom Come, are living across the road from me in Foxgrove Avenue.

Arthur was already a legend by the time he moved to Beckenham. As the Crazy World of Arthur Brown, his stage act involved his entry wearing a flaming headdress, as the band struck up his signature hit, "Fire."

But there was a mishap with the flaming halo during a performance, which resulted one side of Arthur's long brown hair being burned away. And he never managed to repeat the success of Fire. Kingdom Come is Arthur's new band, designed to project him back into the rock limelight.

Soon afterwards I encounter the jazz pianist Keith Tippett and his wife, rock singer Julie "Wheels on Fire" Driscoll. I discover that they live five minutes' walk away in Albemarle Road. This means that my home is triangulated between three musical icons, each representing a totally different strand. Julie has given up solo performance and appears to be very much under the influence of her husband. This is a source of distress to Brian Auger, who tells me he would dearly love her to return to his band and make more hit records.

Still not sure what I want to do with my life – and waiting for a new opportunity to arise – I fall into a groupie groove for a while, following Kingdom Come around to their gigs, but always feeling slightly uneasy about it. I become friends with Arthur and, as we get to know each other, I discover that beneath his outrageous stage persona he is in fact a rather serious, conventional English gent. One evening Angie plays a seduction game with him in front of a room full of people. Instead of going along with it and trading wisecracks, Arthur squirms with embarrassment.

Our days at 24 Foxgrove Road are drawing to a close. Property developers are prowling the leafy outer suburbs, seeking sites where one house split into four apartments can be torn down and replaced with a block of twenty. Number 24 is a prime target and I am in negotiation with a stereotypically smooth bloke over what it's worth to get rid of us.

Impetuous as always, and not thinking through my options with due care and consideration, I agree to a cash settlement. Barry and Christina, also hard up, do the same. The elderly lady living in the flat between us is more astute and chooses to be re-housed.

This lady is a piano teacher, sometimes giving lessons at home. We were subjected to excruciating scales, stumbling renditions of "Für Elise" and wonky arpeggios. This is certainly the reason she never complained about being sandwiched between two lots of amplified folk rock.

By this time Peter Finnigan has moved to Essex and is no longer easily available for the children. I make one of the worst decisions of my life by moving in on a share basis with a local musician who has a large flat – pretty well empty after his girlfriend has moved out. Before I take up residence there I spend some of my developer money on a trip to America with Caroline and Richard.

While I am in the States I hear *Hunky Dory* tracks played on local rock stations and assume that David is finally getting the recognition he deserves.

This turns out not to be the case. He has made a brief trip to America and has finally managed to get out of his contract with Ken Pitt. Angie has extensive show business management contacts, so it seems likely that she is responsible for finding Tony Defries as Ken's replacement. But despite the America sortie and a new manager promising a rapid ascent to stardom, David is still jogging along, little-known but increasingly appreciated by the musical cognoscenti.

At Haddon Hall a new face has taken up residence again. An extremely handsome face framed with long, very blond hair – Mick Ronson. Ronno had previously lived with David and Angie for several months soon after they moved in. He had gone home to Hull and lived with his parents for the past nine months, having no contact with David.

David calls and invites him to join a new musical line-up, which is taking shape as part of a total makeover of David's stage presentation. Ronno is a professional musician whose skills include not only electrifyingly brilliant guitar but also the ability to arrange and score. With Ronno as compadre, David is zeroing in on the formula that will lead to his breakthrough.

The music writer Paul Trynka told me some years later that Defries didn't do much for David until "Oh You Pretty Things," the song he wrote for Peter Noone of Herman's Hermits, which got to number 12 in the charts. "After that," said Trynka, "everyone wanted a piece of the action."

ENTER ZIGGY

In the run-up to the launch of Ziggy Stardust, David is a powerhouse of musical inspiration, Angie's talent in the mix is style and presentation, and Ronno is the foundation stone. I take an instant liking to Mick Ronson. He is a kind and gentle soul, not verbally articulate, but when he picks up a guitar he is mesmerising. Ronno died far too young and is fondly remembered by all who knew him.

In the midst of this supercharged activity a small boy is taking his first steps – eyes full of wonder and closely followed by his nanny who lives in one of the Haddon Hall flats.

Angie is not the epitome of hands-on motherhood, but with my track record I can't be too hard on her for that. Every time I visit, there is a lot going on at Haddon Hall – the place buzzes with activity and excitement. I mooch around feeling redundant, while musicians tune up and practice riffs, Zowie and nanny frolic in the hallway and Angie cooks fry-ups for the hungry hoards.

One day I turn up to find David's appearance transformed. Gone is the long-haired androgynous look. Replacing it is short, snappily cut bright red hair. Enter hairdresser Suzy Fussey, a very good-looking woman who later becomes Mrs. Ronson. When David converts from suburban folkie into

Ziggy Stardust, Angie also changes her hairstyle. She has it cut very short and bleached platinum.

David's personality also undergoes a change around this time. He is more aloof, and visits to Foxgrove Road no longer happen. Until that point it was a friendship between equals, but now it feels like David is slipping into pop star self-importance. With the onset of these airs and graces, those of us who had been in easy-going friendship feel a bit miffed.

Someone told me later that Angie had convinced him that, even before he hit the showbiz stratosphere, David should behave and live as if he were already a star.

Haddon Hall went through a period of rapid change. The messy musicians with their beer, spliffs, ciggies, girlfriends and band paraphernalia were banished to their own flat.

Around this time Ronno was joined by Trevor and Woody, two of his mates from Hull. Ronno and Woody had already played on *The Man Who Sold The World*, with Tony Visconti on bass. Trevor replaced Tony for *Hunky Dory*.

The three musicians from Hull start to rehearse David's new compositions together, coalescing into a band which becomes The Spiders From Mars.

There must be cash in the Bowie piggy bank, because Angie has obviously been on a shopping spree to refurnish the flat. The sitting room is transformed on an art deco opulence theme, with oriental rugs, Tiffany light shades, an ornate carved oak chest, squashy armchairs and an outsize sofa.

On another of my increasingly rare visits I arrive to find that the musical gallery sleepers have been replaced by Freddie Burretti and his girlfriend, Daniella Parmar. I say girlfriend, but both of them are sexually ambiguous and quintessentially trendy. They are the sort of people who can sniff out fame just before it happens, attach themselves to it and make themselves indispensable. After they are in residence for a while the flat exudes a strong odour of decadence.

Apparently David and Angie encountered Freddie and Daniella at a gay nightclub called El Sombrero. This must have happened around the time when gay was starting to become the flavour of the showbiz moment. I think this resonated at a personal level for Angie, who is genuinely bisexual, but in David's case I suspect he saw it as an opportunity rather than something that was embedded in his DNA.

Freddie is a master tailor-dressmaker. He is outstandingly talented and hardworking. Whenever I visit he is busy at his sewing machine or cutting table or fitting Angie with her latest outfit, as well as making the stage costumes for David and the Spiders. Freddie's creations pile up on hangers around the Bowie bedroom – flamboyant, colourful, stylish and undoubtedly very expensive. Angie's flair for style and presentation contributes a lot to this process.

By this time Angie has assumed a *grande dame* persona, looking at me haughtily down her patrician nose and patronising me something rotten. She now has an adorable son, a husband who is about to be idolised by millions – and a personal tailor.

She keeps telling me how much she had learned from me and what a great muse I have been for David, but none of this seems sincere. I feel uneasy in her company and as time goes by I visit less and less frequently.

David is a remote figure by this time, who occasionally comes into the room when I am there but hardly ever speaks to me. The cosy intimacy of our lives at Foxgrove Road is long gone.

I suspect that Tony Defries's influence also contributed to the seismic shift in the Bowie matrix. Tony turned out to be a slippery character, who in classic showbiz style caused a lot of David's hard-earned money to disappear into a black hole – but he was also the dynamo behind the launch of Ziggy Stardust and The Spiders From Mars.

From this time onwards my experience of the Bowie phenomenon is episodic. I am an onlooker rather than a participant.

The curtain comes down on the Beckenham era when David and Angie invite all of us involved in it to a Ziggy performance at the Earls Court Arena in London.

We have guest seats in a prime location and are swept along by the magic of the performance, along with a capacity audience that erupts with enthusiasm after each song and screams for more at the end. It is loud, brash, theatrical and sensual.

David and Ronno, dressed in gaudy satins and silks, swoop and gyrate around and against each other in blatantly sexual manoeuvres. It has absolutely nothing in common with the T-shirt and jeans Three Tuns uniform. David has finally become a rock star. It is an electrifying emotional experience for all of us who appreciated his talent before he entered the hall of fame.

Afterwards David and Angie throw a party at Haddon Hall. Daughter Caroline comes with me, by this time a precocious thirteen-year-old with an interest in boys.

Alongside the Beckenham contingent there is an assortment of London music biz people – performers, DJs and hangers-on – some of whom I recognise from my Fleet Street days. Chelita Secunda for example, a woman with a finely tuned instinct for the latest Big Thing. It is an excellent party with gourmet food and lots of champagne. David is in his Ziggy outfit and Angie wears Chanel – or a Freddie clone thereof.

When Caroline and I get up to leave, David puts an arm round my shoulders and escorts us to the door.

"Goodbye, Mary," he says. "You are a wonderful woman and I will never forget you."

I never see him in person or speak to him again.

AFTERMATH

I have no problem admitting that I was out of my depth in the new environment that surrounded David when Ziggy Stardust exploded into mass popularity. The ego displays, the posturing and the obsequious attitudes manifested by journalists and hangers-on caused me to recoil into my anonymous way of life. I was in fact rather shy in the company of the Bowie entourage from then onwards. I found them intimidating – most of them either ignored me or occasionally condescended to acknowledge my existence.

One exception to this state of affairs was the inimitable Lindsay Kemp, who, more than anyone else in David's mandala, had an absolute right to live and behave like a prima donna. He *is* a prima donna – an outrageously camp exhibitionist on stage and a kind, witty, loyal and egalitarian friend in everyday life. I got to know and love Lindsay while David was revelling in the trappings of rock stardom, and Lindsay was living in a small apartment in Battersea on the south bank of the River Thames.

I went to Lindsay's mime and dance classes at Pineapple Studios in Covent Garden and learned deeply embedded self-expression and confidence from him for the first time in my life. To this day I don't think Lindsay is aware of the impact he had on me. He is a true guru, a genius whose greatest pleasure is to share his realisations with others.

We were also chums and shared a lot of laughs. On one occasion Lindsay was getting ready to attend the opening night of a film of one of his mime performances at the National Film Theatre. We sat alongside each other, doing our makeup at two theatrical mirrors with a halo of lights around them. Lindsay would be making an entrance, so he dressed for the occasion in a huge floppy hat adorned with feathers, ribbons and flowers, a long, slinky satin dress and high heels.

There was no limo to pick him up so we took the number 7 bus. We would have been a centre of attention in the 21st century, but this was the early 1970s. The expressions on the faces of our fellow passengers ranged from dropped jaws through sniggers and big smiles to shocked horror. Needless to say Lindsay remained glamorously unperturbed.

Later in our friendship Lindsay and his stage partner Jack Birkett (known as The Great Orlando) agreed to perform *pro bono* at a benefit event I organised to raise funds for The Prince of Wales Crescent Residents Association, a squatter organisation fighting evictions in Kentish Town, north London. This happened just before Lindsay's first major West End appearance.

The day before he opened at Covent Garden, Lindsay was on the front cover of *The Observer* magazine. He and Jack were also generating enchantment for a gathering of scruffy squatters and their friends at a ramshackle squatted community centre called The Polytantric. We raised £700 which we spent on lawyers, but to no avail. The London Borough of Camden got their eviction orders and Prince of Wales Crescent was bulldozed out of existence.

Lindsay Kemp was head over heels in love with David Bowie and spoke wistfully about the time when David jilted him. Lindsay has a lightning quick brain and stiletto wit, but I never heard him say an unkind word about anyone – and certainly not about David. He was well to the left politically but out of sympathy with the political correctness that was in vogue in the 1970s.

"The poor, the hungry and the homeless need resources more than the queers," I heard him say with a wry smile, while reading about Ken Livingstone's support for a Lesbian action group in Islington.

A BANKABLE BOWIE

From being viewed by the music moguls as too arty and intellectual, suddenly David Bowie was every promoter's dream – a bankable proposition with global potential.

He was on the leading edge of what became known as Glam Rock – in fact, it is probably not far off the mark to say that he invented it. As soon as he started to attract audiences, his flamboyance, ambiguous sexuality and charisma propelled him into stardom.

The pre-teens screamed and swooned for him and the rock cognoscenti heralded him as one of the all-time great performers. Ziggy Stardust was an inspired character, and *The Rise and Fall of Ziggy Stardust and The Spiders From Mars* showcased some of the best songs he has ever written.

Towards the end of David and Angie's time in Beckenham there was a more or less permanent posse of pre-teen girls ensconced on the doorstep at Haddon Hall. Angie was gracious with them, but their home life was no longer private. Soon afterwards they moved to a rented house in Maida Vale, London, and later to Chelsea.

I have to confess that only a few Beckenham Arts Lab people spotted David Bowie as a rising rock star and I was not one of them. Along with many others I was gazing in a different direction, fascinated by Growth as a social experiment. I saw us all as stars. Hubris and naïveté united in the hippie mindset – we really did believe we could change the world, and that potential was much more interesting to me.

David deserved his success – it was a long time coming and he worked very hard to achieve it. In addition to his talent as a composer, he knows how to maintain focus and to constantly re-invent himself. All of this is on record, so there is no need for me to recap.

What has not reached the public domain so far is a detailed, experiential analysis of the period in Beckenham which was, without any doubt, the bedrock of David's trajectory into his iconic status. Every book about him that has been written so far skims over Beckenham and in some cases ignores it completely. This blind spot needs to be illuminated and that is what I hope I've done here.

But that is not the primary intention behind this book. What I most want to clarify is the fact that David and, to a lesser extent, I were catalysts, facilitators and participants in a slice of social history. We set up a situation where the creativity, ingenuity and enthusiasm of a young generation were able to flourish in the mundane environment of a deeply conservative London suburb. For a short period Beckenham woke up and cavorted with us in a freewheeling adventure. It was over almost before it had begun – but it was a spectacular ride while it was in motion.

Any illusions I cherished about putting the Bowie experience into a file marked "history" were dispelled sometime in the mid-70s. My eyes alighted on an item about him almost every time I opened a newspaper. They were mostly long-winded assessments of his global popularity – written by rock aficionado journalists who interpreted the Bowie phenomenon through the lens of their own projections.

Bob Dylan received similar treatment. Both of them were elevated to quasi-religious status – demigods of the rock landscape. David seemed to revel in this adulation. He took part in TV chat shows and spun the publicity plates with statements like, "I am gay and I always have been," which whipped up one media feeding frenzy, and he was seen to give a Nazi-style salute at Victoria Station, which set off another one. Neither of these stunts were a sincere reflection of his sexuality or his politics.

Alongside the seemingly bottomless pit of interest in his role as an entertainer, there was a regular drip-feed of sensational stories about the turbulent state of the Bowie marriage. I suppose it was inevitable that two moody, highly strung individuals like David and Angie would end up tearing each other apart. This is precisely what happened – and it happened in an excruciatingly public arena.

Then the books started to appear and authors started to beat a path to my telephone and/or front door.

I realise now that if you figure in the career path of a star who achieves iconic status and the fame that goes with it, there are always authors, journalists and fans on your case. At first I was generous with my reminiscences, giving time, thought and tidbits of gossip to all who got in touch. Some authors quoted me without speaking to me, resulting in a variety of distortions and misinterpretations, which multiplied and recycled over the years.

One or two authors paid me small fees, which I appreciated. One or two were outraged when I suggested they might like to offer me some money. Eventually I declined to talk to anyone unless we agreed a fee in advance.

I got tired of trotting out the same answers to similar questions:

"What was he like when he was living with you?"

"How did you get on with Angie?"

One of the better literary attempts to penetrate the Bowie myth was the 1987 *Alias David Bowie: a Biography* by a husband and wife team, Peter and Leni Gillman. Peter is a former Fleet Street journalist, so we were more or less on the same wavelength. But even he abandoned any pretence of objectivity and based his story in a personal experience.

Kevin Cann's 2010 book, *Any Day Now: David Bowie, the London Years (1947-1974)*, is probably closest to factual accuracy so far. It is the result of painstaking, detailed research and the timeline treatment is a treasure trove for anyone wanting to check out dates, personalities, influences, collaborators and so on.

I was much more hands-on with the late Kerry Juby, a commercial radio music presenter who embarked on a project to produce a vinyl disc and a book under the rubric *In Other Words... David Bowie*, published in 1987. I helped Kerry find contributors, including Angie, and I flew to Milan on his behalf to interview Lindsay Kemp.

ANGIE RETURNS

I was a single mum and a full-time working journalist with Daniel, my third child born in 1975, living with me in a council flat in Camden Town, north London. I had child minders when I was on shift at London Broadcasting Company/ Independent Radio News (LBC/IRN), but most of the time when I wasn't working I was exhausted.

The leisurely pace of life with the Beckenham Arts Lab was a distant memory. I had no personal contact with David, but Angie kept in touch from time to time.

In the early 80s Angie re-materialised in London, taking up residence in a rented house with her daughter Stacia. It transpired that she was aiming to establish a musical career for herself. She assembled a band, hired rehearsal studios and eventually did a gig. I went along with a friend and we agreed that Angie's performance was not going to catapult her to stardom.

She looked fabulous in magnificent outfits, but her voice was not strong enough to rise above and beyond amplified guitars. She of the willowy, sensual female form stood rooted to one spot for most of her time behind the mike. Her personality and charm were not evident. Angie desperately wanted to be a performer, but the reality appeared to me to be a bad dose of stage fright.

As the years passed I moved from London to Canterbury and then to Bristol with Daniel and ex-husband number two, Magnus Carter.

By the time that marriage was over and Daniel had left Bristol for university in London, it seemed as if I had finally managed to shake off the Bowie hangover – but that idea too, turned out to be a chimera.

The haunting returned in 2001, when Cliff Watkins contacted me with what seemed at first to be a bizarre project. Cliff has a passion for Beckenham history. During his research he came across references to The Three Tuns, the Arts Lab – and the fact that one of the all-time great popular music icons had lived and worked in Beckenham.

Cliff decided that this globally famous local hero should be acknowledged with a plaque, along the same lines as the blue ones that grace the former residences of distinguished Britons. And of course the plaque had to be located on what used to be The Three Tuns.

At that time it was still a pub, but no longer with the same name. It was a Rat & Parrot franchise and the couple who managed it were surprised and delighted when Cliff told them about its illustrious history. They agreed to the installation of the plaque without hesitation – and they offered to host a party to celebrate the occasion.

GROWTH - THE BECKENHAM ARTS LAB HELD A FREE
FESTIVAL HERE ON 19TH OF AUG 1969 FEATURING:
DAVID BOWIE, THE STRAWBS, PETER HORTON,
BRIDGET ST JOHN, APPENDIX PART 1, COMUS,
NITA & DAVE JONES, SUN, AMORY KANE, KAMIRAH,
GILES & ABDUL, CLEM, BRIAN MOORE, KEITH
CHRISTMAS MOX, GEORGE UNDERWOOD, GUN HILL
& DJ TIM GOFF. WITH HELP FROM MARY FINNIGAN,
CALVIN MARK LEE, MARY ANGELA BARNETT, CHAS &
LIZ LIPPEAT, SPUD MURPHY, NICK & MICK GODWIN,
JAMIE PLUMMER, DAVID BEBBINGTON, SAM WHELLER,
DAVE WALKING, BARRY & CHRISTINA JACKSON,
SUZI CARTWRIGHT & NICK JENNINGS

*Local history enthusiasts designed this plaque for the
Recreation Ground bandstand. It was not installed.*

After talking to Cliff I was infected by his enthusiasm and agreed to take part in an unveiling ceremony, alongside Christina Ostrom, formerly Jackson. Our lives had moved on – both of us had new partners and had established careers – me as a broadcast journalist and Christina as an artist, but our friendship stood the test of time. We were very happy to be collaborating again, this time as the centre of attention at the unveiling of a large red plaque that commemorated David Bowie, The Three Tuns, the Beckenham Arts Lab, Haddon Hall and Foxgrove Road.

The plaque event generated a lot of excitement – especially when a folk club graduate, Steve Harley from the band Cockney Rebel, agreed to play a set. The Mayor of Bromley turned up, resplendent in official regalia, Bowie fans crowded around us and the local media were out in force. Christina and I made speeches and together we pulled the cord that unveiled the plaque. My speech included a greeting from David Bowie – but I'm not sure it was genuine.

The most intense emotion surfaced when we discovered several Arts Lab survivors enjoying the party. We fell on each other with delighted squeals and my partner Chris Gilchrist took a photo of Christina and me kissing James Plummer. The festivities continued until closing time with Bowie tribute bands.

Sometime later I heard that The Three Tuns name was restored briefly, before the building was sold off and converted into a pizza restaurant. There's Bowie-themed artwork on the walls and, after a four-year delay, the red plaque is back in place outside. But the echoes of love, peace and radical realignment are long gone. No matter what they try to do to maintain linkage with the past, it's a sterile fast food outlet and the resonance is absent.

Until 2013 I had a holiday from the Bowie hangover – except for a reunion with Angie. She was in London to take part in an event about outsiders and, to my surprise, decided to hop a train and visit us in Bristol.

Chris Gilchrist and I were settling into coupledom at the time, so we entertained Angie to a roast lamb lunch. We had both aged more or less gracefully and had both put on weight. I know it's a cliché, but the years seemed to telescope – apart

Unveiling the plaque with Christina Ostrom

from Angie's fatwa on any mention of The Man. She was her usual ebullient self, still a drama queen and still loudly American.

I admired her for the way she rebuilt her life after the divorce from David. I liked her enthusiasm, her courage and her generosity towards people who needed help, especially people with gender issues. Angie championed the underdog – social misfits, the poor, the oppressed and victims of injustice.

Before she came to see us, we talked on Skype from time to time. During those conversations I learned that David was no longer supporting her financially, that he refused to have anything to do with her and that she was alienated from her son, Zowie/Duncan. She lived in Tucson, Arizona with a partner called Michael who was 17 years her junior.

Angie was gone as fast as she arrived and sometime later turned against me. I was baffled because her grievance was not based in any reality I could identify.

In 2013 London's Victoria and Albert Museum staged "David Bowie Is," an exhibition primarily based in Bowie's extravagant stage costumes and loosely following his life line. It ran for four months in London and later toured the world – an outstanding success commemorated with a huge, lavishly produced coffee table book.

At home in Bristol I heard about the exhibition but didn't feel strongly motivated to see it. That is until Tony Visconti posted a series of photographs and comments on Facebook about the party thrown after the opening night.

I was miffed. Everyone in the UK and from afar who was connected with David Bowie had apparently received an invitation – except for me.

I phoned the organisers. The person I spoke to recognised my name immediately and was suitably apologetic. The V&A was quick to make amends – inviting Chris and me to see the exhibition and have lunch with the curators – Victoria Broakes and Geoffrey Marsh.

David Bowie performing at the Free Festival in 1969

Bowie festival returns

A group of David Bowie fans are reprising the Free Festival at the Recreation Ground, in Croydon Road, Beckenham, on September 15, from 2pm.

The festival was first held 44 years ago and was played by Bowie, who remembers it in his song *Memory of a Free Festival*. Visit facebook.com/beckenham.bowie.

6 | August 15, 2013

MEMORY OF A FREE FESTIVAL

A blast of unexpected magic happened in 2013 when Natasha Ryzhova Lau launched Memory of a Free Festival. I caught up with her initiative via Facebook and immediately offered to help out by taking care of the PR. Natasha is Russian, a fashion designer and a Bowie fan. She had a poster on her bedroom wall in Moscow featuring David playing guitar on the Croydon Road Recreation Ground's Victorian wrought-iron bandstand.

Natasha married and came to live in Beckenham with her husband and young daughter. One day she went for a walk at the Rec and had a eureka moment when she spotted the bandstand. Close inspection revealed that it was dilapidated and badly in need of restoration.

Natasha approached the Friends of Croydon Road Recreation Ground, who told her that, in common with local authorities across the UK, the London Borough of Bromley was operating on an austerity budget and had no resources available to repair the bandstand.

Shocked that this iconic structure was in danger of further decay, she offered to collaborate with The Friends to raise money for a restoration fund. And that is how Memory of a Free Festival 2013 came into being.

Arts Lab oldies reunion at 2013 Memory of a Free Festival, including Pete Missen, Deborah Kent, James Plummer, Mary Finnigan, Bill Liesegang

Natasha took on the organisation of a Bowie-themed music festival alongside her full-time job, childcare and home life. She is a feisty thirty-something with a huge reservoir of charm. I warmed to her from the start.

During preparations for the festival I re-established contact with Amory (Jack) Kane, the American folkie who rejected me in 1969 and who played at the original Free Festival. To my absolute astonishment he volunteered to fly from California at his own expense to perform at MOAFF. I incorporated this development into a news release announcing that David Bowie was contributing signed memorabilia to the auction being held to raise money for the bandstand.

The media ignored Amory but went into a frenzy over David's contribution. Natasha darted about from one studio to another doing interviews and one by one the national newspapers and websites followed each other to run the story. The result was that MOAFF got wall-to-wall publicity, which gave us the exposure we needed both in and around London and with the Bowie fan community.

The South London suburban way of life has gone through many changes since the freestyle 1960s. Bureaucracy around events in public spaces has kept pace with the plethora of regulations that have accumulated over the decades.

Natasha found out quickly that it is not possible to stage a free festival in the noughties – the expenses involved in setting up an event have to be met from day one.

So the reprise of the UK's first-ever free festival was forced to charge a £5 entry fee. It turned out to be extremely good value for money.

On a cool Saturday in September heavy clouds hung over Beckenham and the weather gurus said that rain was inevitable. I met Amory Kane at Beckenham Junction Station the evening before and we talked catch-up over dinner and well past midnight. It was a joyful reunion for both of us. We stayed in separate rooms in the same overpriced B&B, carried on our conversation over breakfast and I drove us to the Rec the next day. It was drizzling when we arrived.

Natasha Ryzhova Lau with Mary at Memory of a Free Festival 2014

Natasha had worked a small miracle, pulling together the strands needed to create a festival atmosphere. There was the bandstand festooned with speakers, microphones, wiring and plug boards and decorated with massed flowers.

The sound man operated out of the back of a car. Water dripped from the leaky roof. There was a master of ceremonies in flowing frock coat and big hat. Musicians tuned their instruments – including Bill Liesegang who was sixteen when he first played on the bandstand on 16 August 1969.

There was a craft market set up in a wide arc around the perimeter of the bandstand arena, there were ice cream stalls, a burger bar, hot and cold drinks, a face-painting lady and 1,500 happy people sheltering under their umbrellas.

Among them were several Arts Lab old timers, including James Plummer, David Bebbington, Chris Leggett, Dave Walkling and Amanda Jennings. It was an overwhelming experience for me to meet up with them again. It felt like a time warp, despite the effects of four decades on our health and appearances.

Natasha managed to persuade a variety of accomplished musicians to perform at MOAFF for lots of fun but no money. Most impressive among them were Raf and O, who kicked off the afternoon. They are a talented avant-garde duo, influenced by David Bowie but not copycat. Bill Liesegang and Amory played loud classic blues together, I was cajoled into making a speech. Natasha almost made me cry when she presented me with a big bouquet.

The Bowie tribute band, The Thin White Duke, kept the energy moving, but it was the finale that swept us into bliss. Tarquin Boyesen was lead singer, D'Arcy Debrett played harmonium, Amory and the rest of the musicians played alongside and Richard O gently but firmly walked me to the microphone to join in the refrain.

And 1,500 voices echoed across the Rec singing Memory of a Free Festival, David Bowie's tribute to 1969, which has become a valedictory anthem to the hippie era.

No amount of sky juice pouring down on us in 2013 could dampen our spirits. It was without doubt one of the best afternoons of my life – equally ecstatic as 1969, if not more so. The energy and enthusiasm of the large contingent of Bowie fans was a contributing factor. Their hero has not toured for many years, following a heart attack in 2004, so any Bowie-related event makes them very happy.

We made £6,950 for the bandstand fund from the auction, donations and ticket sales.

The citizens of Beckenham and Bromley – as well as Bowie fans nationwide – made it clear they hoped the festival would become an annual event. Natasha did not want to carry on as lead organiser. So she handed it over, but the people who picked up the baton made a terrible mess of it.

August 16 2014 was the forty-fifth anniversary of 1969 so it seemed wholly appropriate to have a repeat performance. But as the date grew nearer, nothing happened. There were no posters, no leaflets, no PR and the bandstand was not booked.

By this time a core group of MOAFF enthusiasts had formed around Natasha, most of whom had helped her make 2013 happen. Worried email and telephone exchanges passed between us – and plaintive enquiries from Bowie fans started to appear on Facebook.

To her everlasting credit Natasha relented and agreed to reprise the lead organiser role. The rest of us swung into gear behind her, joined by another 1969 graduate, Roger Wotton, still leading Comus, still writing his quirky, left-field songs but now known as Richard Raven.

It was another delightful day cobbled together at the last minute, but this time held under blue skies and warm sunshine. Because it was organised on an emergency basis, at top speed and minus detailed planning, MOAFF 2014 had a more amateurish feel to it – and also featured most of the performers from the previous year.

But our fans were delighted to be back, and so too was Amory Kane, this time joined by his wife Iris on Hohner accordion and daughter Aurora on trumpet. The Kane trio was the backbone of the final anthem, with Iris's accordion replacing the harmonium. Tarquin did lead vocals again, with me alongside him – a lot less coy than I was a year earlier.

The addition of a beer tent was much appreciated and once again Bowie fans delved into their pockets at the auction. The *pièce de résistance* up for grabs was lunch with Tony Visconti at The Groucho Club in London. It raised £520. Sadly Roger Wotton's set was marred by a breakdown in sound quality, but apart from that hiccup we achieved another successful afternoon.

There is not a scintilla of doubt that MOAFF has the potential to build on its two manifestations so far – but at the time of writing in November 2015, the prognosis for this to happen is not good.

The Friends of the Croydon Road Recreation Ground hold the total of £16,000 raised by the two MOAFFs in their bank account. It was handed over to them with goodwill by Natasha Ryzhova Lau. As plans for an enhanced, more professional MOAFF got underway everyone involved, including me, assumed that the Friends would be willing to allocate £3,000 as a loan from the £16K. We needed it to seed-fund the event in 2016.

Our plan was to take control of the finances but to continue to donate towards the bandstand restoration project. When that was completed we wanted to carry on supporting improvements to other features at the Recreation Ground that are in need of repair.

The Rec is owned by the London Borough of Bromley — a local authority subjected to the savage funding cuts imposed by Britain's Conservative government. There is no money available from Bromley Council, so it seemed a no-brainer to us that The Friends would be delighted to help us launch an annual festival that would provide ongoing cash flow.

It transpired that we made a naïve error of judgment. An approach was made to the Chairman of The Friends, who refused to consider any involvement with MOAFF. This effectively torpedoed our endeavour — strangled it at birth in fact, because the initial expenses involved in setting up a sophisticated public event are way beyond the means of the individuals concerned.

At first we were dumbfounded – how could this man be so mean-spirited and so myopic? But on reflection, I realised that he disliked MOAFF from the start and is far removed in his attitudes from the older people of Beckenham who appreciated The Arts Lab in 1969. It seems the Chairman wants to keep events at the Rec at village fete level.

Our vision for an annual MOAFF was radically more ambitious. In July 2015 Bowie mega-fan and my friend and collaborator Wendy Faulkner (aka Wendy Woo) nudged me into attending the final concert in London of a country-wide tour by a rock supergroup called Holy Holy. The front runners in this magnificent ensemble are former Spider From Mars drummer Mick (Woody) Woodmansey and my old friend Tony Visconti on bass. The band performed David Bowie's album *The Man Who Sold The World* in its entirety during the first half and after the break a collection of early Bowie numbers including some that were written in Foxgrove Road.

Tony and I had lunch together the following day. It was a beautiful reunion. I confessed to an agenda – which was an invitation to Tony to be the music curator for MOAFF 2016. To my delight he accepted. Tony on board, together with the possibility that Holy Holy would headline the festival, elevated its potential to international status – with Bowie fans worldwide eager to spend their spare cash on a trip to Beckenham. Not only did the dinosaur Chairman scupper benefit to the Rec, but he also denied it to the local economy.

Wendy Faulkner, Tony Visconti, Mary Finnigan and Woody Woodmansey at Shepherd's Bush Empire before the final concert in the 2015 Holy Holy tour.

I progressed from trying to shake loose from the Bowie legacy to taking an active role in an event that celebrates his genius. A glimmer of hope remains that MOAFF will continue, but it will need a minor miracle to bring it back to life.

I used to do my best to steer clear of Bowie fans, but now I have made acquaintance with many of them and friends with several. So what caused this change of heart?

David Bowie's shadow has hung over my life for more than forty-five years. I think for much of this time I was in denial about the depth of resentment I felt at being cast aside.

The most unpleasant moments occurred when I realised that he never took me seriously – I was just one of several simultaneous lovers. My home was a convenient place of refuge. I was around when needed – and discarded when no longer useful.

I admit these perspectives are on the cynical end of the scale – he probably did genuinely like me for a while. He probably didn't realise I was so badly hurt when he got together with Angie.

My experience fits neatly into the category marked "path to stardom." So much so that it is a cliché, and that is probably one reason why the bitterness drained away and I realised, "Oh well, so what?"

Lots of people have been invited on board for a while and then been thrown off the rock 'n' rollercoaster – I am just one casualty among many, and the last thing I want is to be remembered as a sourpuss who could not forgive and move on.

There are reasons why I am grateful for my time with David Bowie. He opened my ears all sorts of different types of music – styles and tonalities that I probably wouldn't have encountered with anyone else. Music which has given me intense pleasure ever since. Music which made it possible for me to appreciate unfamiliar genres like North African, Middle Eastern and central Asian, all of which I came to love during an eleven-year role as UK PR person for Morocco's Fes Festival of World Sacred Music.

I guess I should fess up to the fact that I lost my appreciation of David's persona when he morphed from scruffy folkie into pseudo-gay glamour – and I lost it for much of his music after *Ziggy Stardust*. Thankfully the glam period was short-lived and what came after was more provocative and more interesting.

I admire his talent for continuous re-invention and I think I understand the psychology behind it. David learned a lot about being human on the cushion at Samye Ling. He learned about the illusion of a separate self – so the many Davids that manifested during the course of his career illustrate that insight.

This perspective is probably incomprehensible for people who have not been exposed to Buddhist theory and practice. David may even have lost sight of it under the impact of the rock star lifestyle – especially during his cocaine era in Los Angeles – but as far as I'm concerned it de-mystifies the apparent Bowie paradoxes that music commentators love to puzzle over.

And the music? I really did try to like it. Angie gifted me a collection of David's albums from *Ziggy Stardust* through to *Pin Ups*. So I listened and listened again many times… and I simply didn't get it. There are at least two tracks on every LP that I can relate to emotionally, intellectually or both. But there is no genuine connection for me – nothing that makes my heart sing. I loved his early music and still do, but there's only one post-Beckenham song that scores deep grooves every time I hear it and that's "Heroes." In my view it's his all-time best.

Above and beyond all other David Bowie contributions to the quality of my life, I thank him for introducing me to Tibetan Buddhism. Study and practice of this arcane shamanic-Buddhist tradition has become the bedrock of my existence. It kept me sane during a succession of crises, including two years of gruelling breast cancer treatment. Yoga and meditation are not easy, but the rewards generated by practice far exceed the effort involved.

Now I have embraced my past and am nurturing it. I see MOAFF as an echo of the best aspects of the 1960s, an unexpected slice of karma that matured without action on my part. I didn't seek it out, I didn't set it up. I simply merged with the energy it had already generated. I hope that MOAFF or something like it will rise again.

EPILOGUE

Seven am Monday, 11 January 2016. I am dozing into consciousness, waiting for Chris to deliver the tea that will kick-start the day. The BBC's flagship news and current affairs *Today* progamme is on low volume beside the bed.

Suddenly I am supercharged awake, screaming. Stark naked, I tumble downstairs into the meditation room, where Chris is doing his morning stretches.

"He's dead," I screech

"Who's dead?" asks Chris, disgruntled at being disturbed

"David."

"Which David?" Then the penny drops and so does Chris's jaw, an expression of shock and astonishment expanding across his face.

Then the phones start up simultaneously and there's a knock at the door.

One of the calls is from *Today* and the bloke on the doorstep is an ITV cameraman.

I am in high-octane shock, running back upstairs to find a garment, babbling incoherently, devastated, unable to take it in. The radio is telling me he died of liver cancer and that no-one apart from his family and close associates knew he was terminally ill. The *Today* presenter, Justin Webb, is flagging me up as their next guest.

I was on auto pilot answering Justin's questions ten minutes after I knew that a man I loved, respected and admired had succumbed to a gruesome illness, the last stages of which must have been extremely unpleasant. I had no recollection of what I said, except to apologise if I was not entirely coherent.

I listened to the interview on iPlayer some time later to check that I hadn't made an idiot of myself and was relieved to know that broadcasting skills are apparently embedded in my DNA.

On that once-in-a-lifetime Monday morning, Chris threw some clothes on and made coffee and toast for the two of us and the ITV cameraman. He was a polite, unpretentious person – which was a bonus because I made him wait to record his interview while I showered, dressed, did my hair and put on makeup. Bereaved or otherwise, nothing would persuade me to face a TV camera looking like I'd just fallen out of bed.

Again, thanks to the digital immortality of modern times, I reviewed the interview via the ITV web site – and was happy to see that my shock and sadness were obvious.

Meanwhile, Chris was manning the phones, setting up a triage system as he answered – mostly handling two calls at the same time. Both the landline and my mobile rang without respite. My beloved rose to the occasion magnificently. He abandoned going to work that day in order to provide me with backup.

My wonderful PR person, Chantal Cooke, called. Her phones started ringing around 6 am. She ignored them for a while but eventually realised something extraordinary must be happening. We fell into a three-person routine, with Chantal firewalling calls from her end, deploying her PR wisdom to decide which ones to pass on to me via Chris and which to turn down.

"The *Indy* are offering £250 for an 800-word tribute – do you want to do it?"

"Two fifty to talk to *The Sun*?"

And "*Good Morning Britain* want you live tomorrow".

I did back-to-back phone interviews until Chris drove me to Whiteladies Road for the first of two BBC visits that day. I did one recorded-for-TV interview and two live radio slots.

Home again, I closed the office door and put my head into the computer, so I could meet *The Independent*'s 3 pm deadline. Reluctantly, I had to turn down *The Guardian*. Here's what I wrote for the *Indy*:

Slowly emerging from sleep with the Today *programme, suddenly I am galvanised awake. David Bowie is dead. Four days after the release of his latest album* Blackstar *and four days after the publication of my book* Psychedelic Suburbia, *a celebration of the time David and I spent together in the London suburb of Beckenham.*

After the initial shock, I burst into tears as a wave of mixed emotions overwhelmed me. Grief, nostalgia, regret and bewilderment – especially bewilderment, when I realise that he died of cancer, because I am a cancer survivor. I won a reprieve from the disease that strikes such dread when you see the doctor's face and hear the words "I'm afraid I have bad news for you."

The David I knew would almost certainly have taken it in his stride – a shrug perhaps, followed by the inevitable questions about survival chances. But he would not regard death as anything other than a fresh challenge. He might have been curious and re-read The Tibetan Book of the Dead *to get a steer on what was coming. And of course he set about writing* Blackstar.

He knew it would be his last and, now we know this, the message it contains is painfully obvious to all who knew him personally and to everyone who loved him.

I loved him – almost from the moment we swallowed a teaspoonful each from my bottle of tincture of cannabis in April 1969. We talked late into the night and a couple of days later he moved into my home in Beckenham, sharing it with me and my two children. He was supposed to be our lodger, but we never observed lodger-landlady conventions. I responded enthusiastically to an elegantly staged seduction a couple of days after he moved in.

From then onwards we led interlocking lives. We opened a folk club together, which morphed into an arts lab and a great flowering of creative expression followed, from the young people of south London. This summer of love, music and art peaked on 16 August 1969 with The Beckenham Arts Lab's Free Festival. Then, almost as soon as it had begun, this slice of social history was over.

David had a lifelong interest in Tibetan Buddhism. He introduced me to this arcane tradition, which has been of great value to me ever since. It includes a firm conviction that there is a lot more to consciousness than this one life. David and I both knew that when it was all over this time around, there would be something else. His path was to give pleasure to millions for more than 50 years, so I think he has notched up some karmic brownie points.

I am profoundly sad at his passing, but also optimistic that he will have a smooth passage through the after-death state and an auspicious re-birth.

The rest of the day was a blur of non-stop phone interviews with media organisations across the globe until I was hoarse and exhausted. The sheer volume of requests was almost beyond belief – we turned down as many as we accepted. Chris called a halt around tea time because I needed to rest and refresh before going live on BBC Points West TV news. As we left the house I said no thanks to Radio New Zealand – which pained me because, after two enchanted visits, I love NZ.

The next morning a large satellite van parked outside our house before dawn, with one man in it. Another three turned up soon afterwards. Around 8.am I was on air with *Good Morning Britain* for less than two minutes. Psyched up to answer questions about David without bursting into tears, I was thrown off balance when Piers Morgan quizzed me about Angie. The whole operation seemed like a waste of time, effort and resources. I said so to the crew, but it was familiar territory to them and they took it breezily in their stride.

The journalistic feeding frenzy continued for another two weeks. I did an average of four interviews a day before it started to tail off –and I was just one among many people connected with David on the media hit list.

Pause for reflection on how and why I became a focus for so much intensive attention. The 'how' is an easy call. *Psychedelic Suburbia* was published on 8 January, 2016 – timed to coincide with the release of David's latest (last) album *Blackstar* – and his 69th birthday. Serendipitously, the events that unfold in the book took place in 1969.

This synchronicity was probably unique in the history of popular music – and when we homed in on it we had no idea that it would include an element bordering on Shakespearean tragedy.

When we planned our strategy it just seemed like a superb PR opportunity – and it certainly turned out that way. The timing of the book launch in tandem with Chantal's expertise worked like magic – kicking off with a *Today* programme package with Arts Correspondent Colin Paterson – and followed up by all the UK national newspapers.

I spent a day in London doing BBC radio and TV interviews – the former with Radio London's delightful Jo Good and the latter with the equally lovely Sarah Harris.

An extract in *The Independent* worked wonders for my self-esteem, because an upmarket national newspaper would only publish material that measured up to their literary standards.

Headlines elsewhere were predictably sex-obsessed:

Former lover Mary Finnigan lifts the lid on fling with the singer before his rise to fame – Mail Online

I was sleeping with David Bowie and he was sleeping with everyone – The Sun

And hilariously misleading…

I slept with Bowie before he was famous –landlady reveals all in sordid book – The Daily Star

Anyone tempted to buy the book based on this example of tabloid fantasy would have been bitterly disappointed.

The pre-publication PR bonanza peaked on 10 January 2016 with in-depth features in the *Sunday Times*, the *Sunday Express* and the *Sunday Telegraph*. The acute irony of this only became apparent on 11 January, when the world woke up to the devastating news.

In media terms it meant that *Psychedelic Suburbia* and my name were right under editorial noses – the papers were probably still lying around on TV, radio and newspaper desks, so the feeding frenzy should not have come as a big surprise. But I was taken aback by the level of interest, because there are many other more famous and more significant people who lived, loved and worked with David during his long, illustrious career.

The phenomenon of David Bowie's megastar status is the key that unlocks the 'why'. He was a complex personality – at times generously available to friends, chat show hosts, fans and fellow musicians and at times aloof, inaccessible and unpredictable. All this added to his mystique. His honesty about his character flaws, his spiral into addiction and the painful stages of his recovery endeared him to millions of admirers worldwide.

But David achieved a lot more than fame as a musician. He was a uniquely versatile artist – he acted onstage and in films, he danced, he mimed and he had style that no other performer has replicated, let alone surpassed. He absorbed a huge range of influences and mostly he maintained his intellectual and spiritual integrity. David was up there with the all-time greats – his death generated a tsunami of grief and a tidal wave of media interest on the same order of magnitude as the sorrow that swept the planet after John Lennon was murdered.

Angie Bowie's role was the most bizarre example of accidental timing in the surreal period after David's passing. A few days earlier she made a grand entry into TV Channel Five's *Celebrity Big Brother* house, where participants are kept incommunicado with the outside world – spending their time in emotional overload, falling out, making up and complaining about each other.

It is supposed to be entertainment and lots of people must love it but, despite curiosity about Angie, I cringed after five minutes or so and couldn't bear to watch it. So I missed the episode where the producers told her off-camera that David had died – followed by a distressing on-camera case of mistaken identity.

There were occasional periods during the early days after David's passing when normal life resumed. I kept the domestic show on the road – walking to Bristol's trendy shopping zone, Gloucester Road, to buy items like fresh fish from the one of the many independent traders who have turned the area into a magnet for the discerning bourgeoisie. Alighting in Café Ronak for a strong flat white, I am overwhelmed by a sudden wave of sadness – tears pour forth and kind people enquire, "Are you alright, dear?"

Well yes, I am and I'm not – I'm in the throes of conflicting emotions because I am in awe of the way the man managed his final days in the incarnation that was David Bowie.

He knew he was dying, so he wrote the music for a play called Lazarus – the guy that JC raised from the dead. He recorded an album called *Blackstar*, a sombre, unsettling collection of uncompromisingly *avant garde* tracks with lyrics like:

> *Look up here, I'm in heaven*
> *I've got scars that can't be seen*

And

> *Look up here, man, I'm in danger*
> *I've got nothing left to lose...*

... with an equally macabre video to go with it.

He made his last public appearance at the first night of *Lazarus* in New York, looking frail and old. It must have cost him a monumental effort, because a few weeks later he was dead. In contrast, the last official photo was upbeat – a smiling David in a snappy outfit.

The waves of sadness undulated through me for some time. They would catch me unawares with no direct trigger – and they would engulf me when I read an obit or a tribute – or in the car after I'd done a studio interview. Despite the fact that I'd had no direct contact with David since 1973, I felt his passing as acutely as if he was a close friend or family. And so too did millions of people across the planet. As the days passed and the mourning was reported, it became obvious that not only was David idolised as an entertainer – he was loved.

The shrine outside Zizzi,Pizza, formerly The Three Tuns pub, birthplace of Beckenham Arts Lab and David's rise to stardom

Mary with BBC presenter Natalie Graham at the shrine at the Recreation Ground bandstand

Gatherings of tearful fans in Brixton, Bromley, Beckenham and New York were televised into millions of homes – with echoes of similar emotional responses to the loss of John Lennon and Princess Diana.

Shrines sprang up in locations associated with his life and career. There were banks of flowers, balloons, photos, drawings, hand-written tributes, candles, poems and mementos in Brixton where he was born and in New York where he died.

I went on two pilgrimages to Beckenham. The first was with Sarah Harris for BBC London TV News before David left his body. The second was with Natalie Graham and crew for the BBC programme *Inside Out*, after his passing. A similar shrine covered the length of the Zizzi Pizza franchise (formerly The Three Tuns) frontage and another graced the bandstand at The Croydon Road Recreation Ground.

On the morning of 11 January 2016 a vivid rainbow was photographed above New York City. According to Tibetan tradition when a great spirit enters or exits a human body, its light body manifests in our dimension as a rainbow.

I was not privy to David's thoughts and feelings after he left Beckenham, but I know from the voluminous publicity that surrounded his private and public life that he dipped into a variety of esoteric traditions. Despite these explorations – or maybe because of them – I believe his core principles were rooted in Buddhism. Because I am Buddhist myself it seems natural to me that an individual like David who was at ease with himself for most of his life and was not seeking external validation, would prefer the Buddhist doctrine of dependent origination rather than the comfort zone of God the Father.

My speculation around this theme was in some measure confirmed by the announcement from David's family that he asked for his ashes to be scattered in the sea in Bali with a Buddhist ceremony.

I think all of us who knew David personally and his millions of fans worldwide were very sensitive with each other in our shared mourning. I waited more than two weeks before I contacted Tony Visconti. I knew he must have been one of the people who was told about the gravity of David's condition.

Tony said that despite knowing it would happen soon, when David died he was so devastated he could only cope with two interviews. He said he felt like he had lost a brother. I had a book to promote, so for a few weeks I was a media whore.

I felt more like I had lost a child, a precocious child who had brought light into my life for a while and then swung off into the stratosphere.

I hope David Bowie is having an interesting journey through the after-death state and I wish him an auspicious rebirth.